Paul Chase is an amazing man, a gifted minister, and a voice of influence everywhere he goes. He is a living example of his own message: that our role as Christians is to show people who Jesus is. I love his passion, his heart, and his commitment to giving hope to those in need. His book will awaken a godly compassion and faith in your heart, and you will never be the same.

—JUDAH SMITH, LEAD PASTOR OF THE CITY CHURCH
AND *NEW YORK TIMES* BEST-SELLING AUTHOR OF *JESUS IS*

WARNING: *Thru His Eyes* is a passionately written book that is hazardous to mediocre Christianity. It is guaranteed to awaken the heart of any devoted believer out to please God. Authored by a heart touched by the life of God, Pastor Paul Chase's uncompromising approach and description answers the case for humanity's need. He passionately imparts with compassion the "why" behind the "what" of what it means to be an authentic twenty-first-century Christian. His sobering real-life experiences and encounters offer the church answers that will make a difference in the church and in the world.

Thru His Eyes will challenge, impact, and ignite your Christian faith with stories that are compelling and captivating. You will not be able to put this book down once you begin! May this book be "God's tool" to rescue and awaken His church, raising up a new breed of believer so that it may again be said: "Those who have turned the world upside down have come here too!"

—ART SEPULVEDA, SENIOR PASTOR
WORD OF LIFE CHRISTIAN CENTER, HONOLULU, HI

I have known Paul Chase for going on thirty-five years, and during that time I have watched him and his wife, Shoddy, pursue God's will for their lives.

As a leader, Paul presents clear goals that strengthen morale and guide people into appropriate action. As a pastor, Paul is deeply in touch with the life experiences of the individuals under his care. Rather than grow cynical and hardened, Paul has maintained the rare qualities of empathy and compassion.

Because lawlessness is increasing in our world and many people's love will grow cold, we must fend off apathy and reach out to the troubled and the hurting. This book stirs the reader to compassionately respond to the times with effective steps that bring honor to God and give true help to people.

—JEFF PERRY, SENIOR PASTOR
ST. LOUIS FAMILY CHURCH, ST. LOUIS, MO

In ministry and in life, it can be difficult to find people whom you can count on through all of life's ups and downs. But as most of you know, when you do find someone like this, you do your best to appreciate them and support them in the ways that they have supported you.

Pastor Paul Chase has been one of those rare kinds of folks to me. He has been a friend, a brother, and a constant supporter of not only the work of Metro World Child but of me personally.

He and I met over two decades ago, and our hearts were knitted together in our desire to reach the lost with the hope of Jesus Christ. He has stood with me in the garbage dumps of Manila and on the stages of some of the greatest churches in the world. I highly recommend his teaching and writing not only for his insight into Scripture, but because the heart with which it is written is unmatched.

—BILL WILSON, FOUNDER & SENIOR PASTOR
METRO WORLD CHILD

What Can Happen

When You See

What God Sees

What Can Happen

THRU

When You See

HIS

What God Sees

EYES

Paul Chase

Compassion: The Most Powerful Force in the World

HONOR✠NET

PUBLISHERS

Sapulpa, OK

Thru His Eyes: What Can Happen When You See What God Sees

ISBN: 978-1-938021-31-2

Published by HonorNet
PO Box 910
Sapulpa, OK 74067
www.HonorNet.net

Lena,

When we see what
God sees, it's hard
for our lives to
remain the same.

Ephesians 1:18-19

Pastor Paul Clark
8-17-14

A WORD FROM THE PUBLISHER...

I have always asked God to allow me to be a *paraclete* (one called alongside to help) to His servants who have a message that the body of Christ needs to hear. I find myself drawn to these seasoned warriors whose earthly exploits will only be known in the halls and portals of heaven, and the masses that eternally reside there because of their relentless service to our King here on earth. These warriors think or take nothing for themselves. They never enter battle for personal glory, fame, or to build any earthly kingdom. They quietly and humbly spread the name and fame of Jesus to all they come in contact with. Little by little, year by year; families, communities, cities and—for those who serve long enough—nations are changed. Paul Chase is such a warrior. In words he would never say, he is a general in God's army of service.

I was introduced to the ministry and fruit of Pastor Paul in the early '90s on one of my first trips to the Philippines. Over the years my contact has been with the fruit of his ministry more than him. People, pastors, missionaries, and people that I would meet from the Philippines and surrounding countries over the years all seemed to have been touched somehow by Pastor Paul's service. I have come to the realization that this is the sign of a world changer. Their ministries are not about their person (self) but about the people (others) they serve. They see things not with their earthly eyes but have vision with a heavenly purpose. They see *Thru His Eyes*. I remember Pastor Paul saying, "If we see what He sees, we will hear what He hears, and then we will touch what He touches. We are His plan to spread His love and life-changing power to the entire world one soul at a time." Then he spoke the words that branded my heart forever. He said, "It is impossible to see what God sees and not be changed. Your heart will never be your own again."

There is no greater example of this in action than what happened in November of 2013. As we were entering into the final editing stages of this book *Thru His Eyes*, Typhoon Haiyan (called Yolanda in the Philippines) hit landfall on November 8, 2013, with ground zero being the city of Tacloban on the eastern coast of the Philippines. Ripping through Southeast Asia, it is now known as the strongest storm ever recorded on earth. With sustained winds clocked at over 200 mph, it wreaked life-altering devastation on the people and landscape in its path. Thousands of people were instantly killed by the death wave of wind and water that swept over them. Tens of thousands more were left with absolutely nothing—no homes or even water or food for the day.

With one of his churches under eight feet of water and everything destroyed by the storm, Pastor Paul and the thousands of congregants from the other forty New Life churches across the Philippines saw what God saw. Pastor Paul and the people of New Life were standing between life and death, choosing to see what God sees so they could touch what God touches. They were enabled to respond because of churches and people from all over the world who supplied the money, vehicles, food, and equipment needed to meet the urgent needs of the Tacloban community. Months later, Pastor Paul and his team are still standing, touching, and committed to feeding over 6,000 schoolchildren a day from the mobile kitchen they built to help meet the needs of the communities. These people were not changed only by the greatest storm on earth but by compassion—the most powerful force in the world—because people chose to see *Thru His Eyes.*

My prayer for you is that after you read this book, your heart will never be your own again, and your world will be forever altered as you experience *What Can Happen When You See What God Sees.*

Thru His Eyes,

Jake Jones
Publisher,
HonorNet Publishers

ACKNOWLEDGMENTS

To my wife, Shoddy, who suffered through untold hours of editing to ensure these words would be direct, encouraging, and challenging, yet never harsh, critical, judgmental, or demeaning in any way. You also helped me greatly in areas where I had a tendency to be ridiculously redundant. Thank you, my love—you're the best.

To Sheryl, Andrell, Betsy, Don, Karen, Jake, and all who made this book possible. It has been years in the making and is most likely overdue. For all the love, support, patience, diligence, encouragement, hours of editing, prayer, and belief in this book, I thank you. You believed these words needed to be put into print and would help others. Without your efforts and support, this book would not be. Thank you.

To my friends who wrote endorsements and the forward to this book: how very much I appreciate your gracious words. Thank you.

To the people of New Life: thank you, thank you, thank you.

To Jesus: thank You for continuing to open my eyes.

CONTENTS

FOREWORD

God has allowed me the privilege of personally knowing many world-changers in my lifetime. One of the most remarkable individuals I have met—and one to whom I personally relate—is Paul Chase, the author of the book you now hold in your hands. Paul heard the call of God when he was a younger man and followed that call to a faraway land to pursue adventures in God beyond anything he ever would have dreamed possible. When his journey began, he didn't know it would become a lifelong preoccupation. Yet more than three decades later, Paul is still living on the foreign soil where God called him, and he will most likely live there until the conclusion of his race of faith.

In 1980 Paul and his young wife, Shoddy, moved to the Philippines in pursuit of the call of God. At that time, neither of them knew they would lead a major ministry among the people of the Philippine islands. Similar to Abraham of old, Paul and Shoddy simply followed the call of God, not knowing what would be required of them, what

God would ask them to do there, or how long their journey would last. As they took those early steps of faith and many subsequent steps in the years that followed, God was watching and testing them to see if they could be trusted with a substantial responsibility in that new land.

Only 2 percent of people who move to the mission field stay twenty years or more. With every year that is added, the percentage drastically drops. So when I first met Paul Chase and heard how long his family had lived in Manila and all that God was doing through them, I felt an instant connection. As I learned more about their Manila-based church, their ministry to the poor, their outreach to the destitute, and their work among people who have been ravaged by natural disasters, my heart rose up to salute them! The Chases not only preach what they believe, but they have also demonstrated it by their lives. All of this gives Paul a strong platform from which to write this book entitled *Thru His Eyes*.

As one who has lived on the front lines and seen the worst with his own eyes, Paul's heart cry is for believers to accept God's call to proclaim the gospel message, starting with where they live. He eloquently describes God's desire for us to see the world around us through the compassionate eyes of Jesus and to reach beyond ourselves with His power through the gospel. Doing so will reverse the curse of darkness and cause the hearers to be able to see the glory of God in the face of Christ.

Chase compels us to be available to make a difference. Ministry to others is not a Sunday-morning thing or a Sunday-night thing. It is a lifestyle that the church is supposed to follow every day of the week. Wherever we are, we possess what the wounded, naked, half-dead people out there need. The only way it is going to get to them is for us to see their needs and allow compassion to motivate us to go to them and pour into their lives.

This is the call that God extends to believers who are serious about obeying Jesus. The questions that Paul poses to each of us in this book are these: Will we see what He sees? Will we hear what God is saying to us? And if we will, are we willing to push aside our creature comforts and rise up to obey Him? If anyone is qualified to ask us these questions, it is Paul Chase, hence the reason God has asked him and not someone else to write this book. I encourage you to read these pages fully. Digest the words, and let them sink deep into your heart and soul. A lost and hurting world is awaiting your response.

—RICK RENNER, SENIOR PASTOR
MOSCOW GOOD NEWS CHURCH, MOSCOW, RUSSIA

INTRODUCTION

Thru His Eyes is my journey of waking up and really seeing the value of people all around me. They were there all along, but not until God opened my eyes did I truly notice them. Prior to this, the majority of people were out of focus and distant. I guess I had myopia, but like the song says, "I can see clearly now." By God's grace, this book is an attempt to relay to you what I now see vividly "through His eyes" and to help you see these things as well.

If your eyes have been shut far too long, I pray this book will stir you and awaken you to the point that you will never be drowsy and fall asleep again. By seeing clearly, we stumble less and navigate life more easily. So what do I see now that I once was blind to? I see people and their needs, and I also realize that to know anything about God, we must understand that His love truly sees and comprehends the needs of others.

I met Christ anew when I started seeing people though His eyes. I have always known He loved me, but now I see just how deeply and utterly in love Jesus is with me—and everyone else, including *you*. He *really* loves us! I pray that you would truly comprehend the length, the breadth, the depth, and the height of this tremendous love He has for you.

When He touches us, we turn around and face what was once at our backs. This changes us. We will never, ever, be the same again. Until we learn how to see through His eyes, we will only see through our own physical eyes. In this state we often fail to step beyond the fears and restrictions that prevent us from reaching out. Jesus, however, came and saw and was *moved* with compassion. That force of love brought change to everyone around Him. What we see through His eyes will stir us and determine how we pray and whom we touch.

I believe our Christian walk is meant to be an adventure of God-filled memories, "heart" photos of all the lives we have touched. Helping others brings a richness and fulfillment to these people, but it enhances our own lives as well, adding meaning, worth, and joy. This book is an invitation to a life that becomes rich through learning how to give. I believe it is time for us to wake up and make the best of the days we have, enjoying the opportunities to see Him expressed through us to our world.

CHAPTER 1

WAKING UP!

*Therefore He says, **Awake**, O sleeper, and arise from the
dead, and Christ shall shine (make day dawn) upon you
and give you light. Look carefully then how you walk!
Live purposefully and worthily and accurately, not as
the unwise and witless, but as wise (sensible, intelligent
people), making the very most of the time [buying up each
opportunity], because the days are evil. Therefore do not
be vague and thoughtless and foolish, but understanding
and firmly grasping what the will of the Lord is.*

—EPHESIANS 5:14–17, AMP (EMPHASIS ADDED)

Most of us in everyday life deal with an alarm clock.
Strange name, isn't it? It is not called a "good-morning
clock" or a "time-to-wake-up clock," but an alarm clock.
The really good ones are loud and obnoxious so as to

wake us from deep hibernation and dream land. Of course, there is the snooze button, which we can push over and over for another hour if needed. I do not know about you, but I prefer to wake up peacefully and not by a mind-jarring alarm. Unfortunately, however, an alarm is often necessary so we do not oversleep and awake in a panic, causing us to run behind schedule. The alarm clock is good for jarring the flesh; it does nothing for the slumbering part of my will, which desperately grips the mattress.

Ephesians 5:14–17 is calling us to wake up, collect our faculties, and become aware of our surroundings. It is saying, "Open your eyes. Use your ears. Let your senses begin to function and communicate messages until your head is awake and you are aware of the decisions you are making."

There are decisions we need to make that affect the world in which we live, but that will not happen if we stay asleep. Once awake, light and illumination will come to us! That means the lights are on, and our eyes can begin to focus. We come out of the fog and can walk with insight and perception. Then our decisions and steps will be solid and secure.

I want to encourage you to stop pushing the snooze button of your life! When snoozing, we are in that half-awake/half-asleep state, an almost semiconscious place where our eyes are closed and we have not yet made a commitment to rise. This is also known as WST, or "wakefulness-sleep transition." Once awake and our eyes are open, however, we still must make the decision to get up. Until that decision is made, nothing much will change.

Sleep can be defined as a natural periodic state of rest for the mind and body in which the eyes are closed and consciousness is completely or partially lost. While we sleep, we are in a state of inactivity, resembling unconsciousness, dormancy, hibernation, or death. In other words, we are alive and breathing, but there is no awareness, alertness, or physical activity. The mind is shut down and decisions are on hold. The body is going nowhere.

A sleeping believer has no effect on his or her world, and I declare that we have rested enough! It is time to take a stand, lay hold of the will of God, and walk it out. The time is here to live a life that boldly declares, "I know God! This is who He has made me, and this is how He wants me to live!"

God told the prophet Joel, *Proclaim this among the nations: 'Prepare for war! Wake up the mighty men, let all the men of war draw near, let them come up'* (Joel 3:9). Joel called the people of Israel to be aware and prepared for the turning of events. It was time for Israel to awaken, stand up, and be strong as a people prepared for battle. If there is anything an enemy wants, it is to come upon a person while he or she is sleeping and catch that person unaware. We need to be awake and alert with wisdom and insight for we live in difficult times. Challenges surround us as we fight for the souls of men and women. We must wake up and become the answer to their cry for help.

Stir Up God's Love in You!

This book is about stirring up the love and compassion of God that reside in you, that will cause you to live life on an entirely different level. At this new level, we can all kiss good-bye any part of our Christianity that is drowsy and boring. It is time to stand, awaking to righteousness and the abounding grace of God in our lives that gives us that ability. The apostle Paul put it this way: *Stand fast therefore in the liberty by which Christ hath made us free, and do not be entangled again with the yoke of bondage* (Gal. 5:1).

One important thing to note is that the strength of our stand is a result of who we are in Christ and is not due to our religious performance, as our enemy would have us think. In Paul's letter to the church at Ephesus, he told the believers to *stand against the wiles of the devil...and having done all, to stand. Stand therefore, having girded your waist with truth* (Eph. 6:11, 13–14).

Standing signifies a transition from sitting—moving from a position of leisure and rest to a position of readiness and stability. The only problem is the church is too often still asleep. Sleepiness can be produced by too much sitting around and inactivity. The call to wake up is a call to return from obscurity and inactivity. But it is more than that; we must also *arise!* In life, we need to do more than just exist in the present moment; we need to carry a presence in the moment that is attentive and walks with purpose. We need to walk and live purposefully, worthily, and with accuracy as wise and intelligent people.

Over two thousand years ago, Paul wrote to the church in Rome these persuasive words: *Besides this you know what [a critical] hour this is, how it is high time now for you to wake up out of your sleep (rouse to reality). For salvation (final deliverance) is nearer to us now than when we first believed (adhered to, trusted in, and relied on Christ, the Messiah)* (Rom. 13:11, AMP). If it was time for the church at Ephesus to wake up to the reality they lived in and to take a stand two thousand years ago, how vital it is for us to wake up today! The bed can be a place of refreshing and healing, but it can also become a place of retreat and surrender where we allow depression and heaviness to weigh upon us as we look to escape in our slumber. Let us not give in to that!

I believe the Spirit of God wants to stir our hearts and awaken us to who we are in Christ, who He has made us to be, and what He has deposited within us. He wants that deposit to begin to flow through us to the people around us. Whatever condition we may find ourselves in, it is not too late to come alive. What Jesus has accomplished in our lives and how He desires to demonstrate Himself through us gives us the ability to progress beyond our present state.

Life is short; it goes by fast! I want to live life well. I want my life to make a positive difference in the lives of others. I do not want to live in response to external demands or pressures put on me by others who try to obligate me with religious expectation. I want to awaken and rise up to the life and love of God inside me! I want my life to enrich others. It is my hope that you do also.

I love my family with all my heart. My lesser loves are riding my Harley and scuba diving. These are some of the great joys in my life, but one of my greatest joys is being able to affect people—not merely in the present but for eternity.

There are believers all over the world whose lives are making a positive impact. I want you to be one of them. I do not believe there is a richer reward in life than when we see our lives touch people near to us as well as those who come across our path. Life becomes a great adventure when we release the love of God to others, allowing them to come into contact with Jesus through our lives in an authentic way.

A State of Being Half Asleep

I am convinced that many people in the church are unaware of the serious conditions that exist in their world. They seem to have been hypnotized by the devil's lie that they are not good enough, strong enough, or gifted enough to become part of the answer to the problems with which people are struggling all around them. It is clear that the enemy works hard to have us shut our eyes in sleep so we will not see the needs around us. We need to wake up and refuse to allow our fears, failures, insecurities, hurts, disappointments, regrets, anger, or guilt to define or disqualify us. Christ wants us to live purposefully and accurately. This kind of living cannot be contained; it will automatically overflow and spill upon the people around us. Why should we allow any more of our days, weeks, or months to be stolen from us? Moses said in Psalm 90:12, *So teach us to number our days, that we may gain a heart of wisdom.* Our days matter.

Love God and Love People

A disciple who continues in God's Word comes to know the truth. Knowing truth brings freedom, freedom brings joy, and joy brings strength. It is critical that we wake up and become aware of the freedom, joy, and strength for which the world is crying out. The Bible tells us, *His compassions fail not. They are new every morning; great is Your faithfulness* (Lam. 3:22–23). I awake daily to the mercies of God and His faithfulness, and so do you. Now it is time to walk in the light of that faithfulness and mercy. We can live as wise, sensible, and intelligent people, buying up time and making the most of the opportunities that come across our paths. These opportunities always involve people. Only two things in life are eternal:

God and people. We need to love both. Loving God is easy. As I am sure you have noticed, loving people is the challenge.

The world is searching for answers, and many are looking in the wrong places. Seeking to deaden their shame and guilt, many drown themselves in a bottle of alcohol or try to escape their pain with drugs or other addictions. People are hurt, broken, and wounded because of unfair and unkind experiences in life. That pain may be the consequence of their own wrong choices, or it may stem from other people's decisions. Either way, our world is full of neglected and damaged people.

If we were to see a man who had just lost half his business, whose home had been put up for sale, whose cars were being repossessed, and who felt like a total failure, we could see the turmoil and pain in his life. At one time a man like this probably would have basked in the light of financial security, but with one downward movement of the economy, he had lost everything. Where does a person like this turn for help?

It seems that everywhere we look these days—not only in our own city or nation, but also throughout the world—we see people suffering physically, mentally, emotionally, spiritually, and financially. People are losing their jobs, many are coming out of college and cannot find a job, the moral values of our culture are crumbling, traditions are being ignored, and our world is just one push of a button away from utter chaos. What is it going to take for us to show God's compassion to our world that is drowning in waves of uncertainty, pain, and panic? It will take a brand-new demonstration of the love of God. It is going to take people like you and me who are willing to tell the world what we have experienced at the feet of Jesus.

We, the church, have an answer! We have been transformed by the Word of God. As carriers of God's love message to the world, we have the God-given responsibility not to just feel the world's pain, but to bring change to those around us. We need a fresh revolution and revelation of God's compassionate love. When this type of love comes on the scene, things change!

Out of the Pew and into Our World

As the community of believers, the church should be a safe place for all people to be loved, accepted, encouraged, and instructed in righteousness. We do not come into the church to hide from the world but to be healed from what has happened to us in our world—for us to be restored, refreshed, rebuilt, and renewed. In this place of His presence, we receive purpose. We learn and grow, and then we are to go back into our world as agents of change to pray for and help everyone, including the poor and needy ones in our communities. Our prayers should be fervent, followed by passionate actions. The time has come for us to break out of our comfortable buildings and places of refuge to engage the world with God's love. Jesus calls us to "come to Him," then commands us to "go to them." (See Matthew 11:28; 28:19.)

Many of us are praying to have a ministry when we already have opportunities to minister every day—namely to our family, friends, neighbors, coworkers, and the people we encounter as we go about our lives. These opportunities to minister life are all around us. I do not want my main focus in life to be one of self-preservation. Jesus did not come for Himself, and the church does not exist to serve itself. In fact, Jesus said, *[I] did not come to be served, but **to serve***

(Matt. 20:28, emphasis added). When Jesus defined His purpose in that way, He also defined ours as His body. It does not get much clearer than that.

What more do we need to motivate us to reach out to others? How many times are we going to see that same hopeless and hurting person and yet say nothing? How many times are we going to be around that same desperate situation and do nothing about it? How long will it take us before we know what to do when we feel people's pain? What is it that holds us back? This book endeavors to answer these questions.

We want the influence of our Christianity to expand—not shrink—in its ability to affect our world and the people in it. We have to focus on more than just what God has done for us. It is time to be consumed with what He has done in us and desires to do through us to touch and meet the needs of this world. We are to be His epistles, seen and read by all with whom we come into contact. (See 2 Corinthians 3:2.)

We know the pathway to help people get out of the ditch of their addictions and helplessness. We have the solution to the problems of the tortured souls around us. We carry the answer to the questions the world is asking. That answer is not religion; it is a person, and His name is Jesus! We are not called to be spectators in life; we are called to be players. Let us stop watching life pass before us; let us get out of the bleachers and onto the playing field. *The Great Commission tells us to "go," while the Great Commandment tells us to "love."* This duality of commission and commandment is the divine answer.

We have the power to stir up faith in others by the power of our own testimony. The same Jesus who loved you all the way to your own victory is the One from whom people need to receive love and who will lead them out of bondage into liberty. The world will be drawn to God when they see acts of compassion demonstrated by His people.

The Ministry of Jesus

The Son of God stepped onto this stage of human activity and despair preaching the good news of the kingdom and offering spiritual life to all who would reach out in faith. This new life could not be purchased by the wealth of the rich or attained by the position of the elite. It could only be received as a free gift by those who would humble themselves to accept it by faith. It is God's grace that makes His kingdom available to us today, and it is faith that gives us access to this amazing grace. We do not earn, deserve, or work for this grace; it is offered freely.

Jesus was tireless in His pursuit to bring hope to the hopeless, healing to the sick, an inheritance to the disinherited, and acceptance to the rejected. His strategy was to empower and transform the company of the disenfranchised and to send them forth with the message of God's love.

We should not be surprised by His deep compassion for those who lived on the fringes of human existence. He came for the least, the last, and the lost. Jesus came in the Spirit of His Father and was anointed to accomplish the Father's will: *God anointed Jesus of Nazareth with the Holy Spirit and with power, who **went about doing good and healing** all who were oppressed by the devil, for God was with Him* (Acts 10:38, emphasis added).

Notice in this verse that the Bible does not say that Jesus went about healing all who were sick but all who were *oppressed* of the devil. Sickness is an oppression of the physical body. Torment, heaviness, worry, fear, and anxiety are all oppression of the soul. The soul—composed of our mind, will, and emotions—is the main target of the enemy. He seeks to confuse our minds, weaken our wills, and corrupt our emotions.

Jesus went about healing those who were oppressed, touching them in every area of their lives—spiritually, physically, and mentally. What motivated Him to reach out to others? *Compassion!* Love was the driving force in His life. His ability to see through the Father's eyes allowed Him to see not only the physical needs but also the spiritual and emotional needs of those He encountered. And when Jesus came into contact with them, He was moved, motivated, and stimulated by love to set them free. The devil has oppressed people with every kind of bondage. They need to be and can be free. The only way they are ever going to be totally free of satanic oppression, however, is by hearing the Word of God proclaimed by people who will speak it with boldness and authority, who are infused with the same love that moved Jesus.

Jesus's mission to heal all those who are oppressed of the devil has never changed. The only difference is that today, He has given *us* that responsibility. He has anointed us by His Spirit with power and the authority to carry on that same ministry of touching people and changing lives. We are His eyes. He gives us the ability to see all three areas of need in mankind. When we discern the physical, mental, and spiritual needs, we can reach, respond, and touch people in His name. This is compassion in action. The apostle John said it powerfully: *As He is, so are we in this world* (1 John 4:17).

We Are the Harvesters

Then He said to His disciples, 'The harvest truly is plentiful, but the laborers are few. Therefore pray the Lord of the harvest to send out laborers into His harvest' (Matt. 9:37–38). The harvest is the Lord's, and we are the harvesters. He sends us to reap where seed has been sown. How are we sent? The compassion of God rises up inside us and becomes more real in our heart than the excuses or insecurities that come to our heads. The loving grace of God for those who hurt, are in pain and sorrow, and who have suffered great loss becomes more important to us than our fear of failure, shame, or rejection.

When the love of God takes hold of us and we see people as Christ sees them, nothing can stand against it or prevent us from loving people with His love. Neither fear, nor ego, nor doubt can be exalted above a revelation of God's kindness; it will motivate us to reach out to those next to us. Why? Because if we do not lend a helping hand, who will? If we do not manifest God's amazing goodness to the world, who will? We are a community of believers. We are the body of Christ. We should not be a bunch of wimps and whiners going through the world thinking, "Oh, I could never get involved in other people's problems." Why not? What is stopping us? Let me ask you personally, what fear lurks in your inner core that could possibly be stronger than the love of God that has filled you?

So what if people talk about you? What does it matter if they think you are crazy? When the dynamics of God's love take hold of you and you finally understand that you possess the secret to others' healing and deliverance, you will not care what people think or say. On the other hand, we do not approach people in pride and arrogance but with the same humility Jesus expressed. We are not to judge people's sin and act repulsed by their conditions or actions. Why would we? After all, remember where *we* came from!

The bottom line is that we are to move alongside the hurting to show them the tenderness of God through what we say and what we do. We are not hindered by the fact that we might not have all the answers. We are emboldened by the Spirit of God within us who is waiting to be displayed through us. We are a conduit, an avenue to be used. Each of us should be like a bunch of live wires waiting to light up people as soon as they come into contact with us.

When we are invited to step into people's lives to help them with their problems, often we will find that their mother, father, sister, brother, grandmother, grandfather, niece, nephew, cousin, or somebody somewhere along the line is a believer who has been praying for them, talking to them, witnessing to them. Somebody has been sowing seeds and has paved the way. Now God is saying to us, "I need someone to reap, someone to harvest." In the time of harvest, reapers are the people with grace and goodwill. They might not have sown the seeds, but, in the perfect timing of God, they are there to reap a harvest of saved lives. God sees souls as the precious fruit of the earth, and His love is the key to harvest time!

We must get our eyes off ourselves to see what Christ sees and be willing to allow God to use us. When we do, the wounded, the scattered, the broken down, the lost, the hurting, and the sick can be cleaned up, healed, and restored. Are you willing to allow God's love in you to be a greater factor in your decisions than your fears? Are you willing to become so overwhelmed with compassion that you forget all thoughts of rejection, failure, or disappointment? Look! The fields are already white unto harvest. Are you willing to be one of God's harvesters? God has no plan, but to reach and rescue the souls of men with the gospel. *You and I,* my friend, are the answer.

"Lord, I Have a Problem!"

The first time my compassion was aroused for those outside the church, I was in Bible school. It was there that I met Jeff Perry, and he had a huge impact on my life. Jeff now pastors a thriving church in St. Louis, Missouri, and it carries that same heart of compassion that I observed in him firsthand beginning in 1979.

Jeff had passion, boldness, and confidence to go out to the streets to tell people about Jesus—not just during the day, but also at night. He would search for the pimps, prostitutes, and others on the less-than-desirable side of Tulsa—usually outside the bars. He would tell these broken people that Jesus loved them, had a plan for their lives, and did not come to condemn them. I would go with Jeff, and it was with him that I learned to step out, reach out, and speak up.

Jeff's boldness caused me to make a decision to confront my fear and not allow it to become a limitation or an excuse. I realized that my love for God and people needed to be greater than my fear of failure, ridicule, or rejection. We had some great adventures as we watched God transform people's lives and mine as well. Jeff was (and is) a real harvester. Watching him, I witnessed prostitutes, bikers, and drunks stumble out of the bars to sit on curbs and thank us for telling them they were loved. I believe God even anointed me to play pool in a gay bar one night for two and a half hours. I could not lose. As long as I was playing, I had the opportunity to talk to the people about Jesus and His love for them. It was exhilarating.

One night, Jeff walked up to a group of bikers outside a bar and started giving them gospel tracts. The biggest guy in the group slapped them out of Jeff's hands and said, "Go away, little man."

I thought, "Hey, that's OK with me. I'm out of here!"

But Jeff looked at him and said, "Are you afraid to hear what I have to say?"

At that point I thought, "So this is where we die."

This dinosaur of a guy replied, "Go ahead, what you got to say?"

Jeff took five minutes and shared the love of God with those guys in the parking lot. Then he closed the conversation with these words: "Now bow your heads and let me pray for you."

When they lifted their heads, they all thanked Jeff and shook his hand. I will never forget that night. The love of God won over fear and intimidation, and the good news was deposited into the lives of those men. The life and love of God in Jeff was greater than the fear in them. That night my own heart was enlarged by being there and watching my friend respond to the love of God by seeking out the lost. I discovered that when sinners see Jesus in our actions and hear His acceptance in our words, they will fall in love with Him. When you become an avenue of Christ, you become invisible, and people are drawn to Him. It is His love flowing through you. This is what compassion does.

"Lord, Give Me a Heart of Love"

Years later, when I first moved to the Philippines, I traveled all over the nation, holding seminars and teaching pastors. I was regularly ministering to hundreds of pastors everywhere. However, I was not doing any evangelistic work at the time, which was fine with me. I was comfortable teaching in churches, Bible schools, and at conventions, but I realized that I was not concerned enough about those outside the church. So I began to pray and ask God to give me a heart of compassion for them.

I prayed, "Lord, I have a problem. I really have no burden for the lost. I minister to pastors and church leaders, but I have no desire to evangelize and preach in the cities and on the islands. I am so comfortable and happy teaching spiritual leaders, but I do not have a heart for the lost."

When I confessed and repented for not allowing God's heart for the lost to consume me, God awakened in me a longing to be used as His vessel to touch people in a totally different way. At this point I prayed, "Lord, give me tears for the hurting, the wounded, and the lost. Give me a heart of love, so I am moved to step out of my comfort zone."

We must be careful that in the busyness and routine of life, ministry, and doing good works, we do not let our hearts become insensitive to the lost. As you walk with God, He will enlarge your heart, and His grace will bring new desires and new directions. He will stretch, challenge, and then empower you. As I prayed, God kept working on my heart. Although I was comfortable, content, and guilt free because I had been obeying God in my ministry at that time, there was no denying I was entering a new season in my life. When this realization hit me, I began to cry out fervently to God, "Lord, let my compassion be greater than my fears. Let me see others as You see them. I want Your eyes."

I had to start with that prayer. The thought of standing in an open plaza and preaching to thousands of people almost gave me a heart attack. I intensified my praying. I felt I was on a mission from God and could not resist the prompting of the Spirit. I dealt with my fears, reservations, and also my excuses. I opened up my heart to the love of God as I asked Him to funnel that love through me, and God answered my prayers. He put within me a heart of compassion, and it began to take me places I had never gone before. He strengthened me to say things I had never said and enabled me to see things I never had dreamed of.

It is important to realize that we may have a message in our heads, but we need the Word that is living in our hearts. To this very day I am still in hot pursuit of this pathway. As God began to bring forth this love in my heart in a deeper way, love—not fear — began to move me. Fear often strikes us hardest when we are faced with the unknown or the uncomfortable, but when God begins to touch our hearts and reach inside us to stir up compassion, we are motivated to do more than just feel sympathy for others in need. We are moved to help bring change to their lives and circumstances. We are compelled by the love of God, which is shed abroad in our hearts by the Holy Ghost. (See Romans 5:5.)

The Gospels say in many places that when Jesus saw people, He was moved with compassion. In response to my prayer, He began opening my eyes to see as He saw. I began to realize how many people had no one to lead, feed, direct, guide, or help them. They were confused. They were distressed, harassed, dejected, and help-less. They were like sheep without a shepherd. (See Matthew 9:36.) As that reality troubled Jesus, it began to trouble me. Why? I was waking up and becoming aware that the hurting and broken people I saw were in the same condition as I had been before I met Jesus! At one time, *I* was the lost, the confused, the distressed, and the helpless. So were you.

CHAPTER 2

EIGHT WORDS

Do all things without complaining and disputing, that
you may become blameless and harmless, children of
God without fault in the midst of a crooked and perverse
generation, among whom you shine as lights in the world.

—Philippians 2:14–15

I am so glad that someone was willing to step into my life to be an answer to my questions and pain. That day was the beginning of a brand-new life for me, and it all started when a young lady spoke eight powerful words to me.

I was working in a large hotel in Florida at a café-type bar. One day a beautiful young lady walked up to the bar, ordered a coke, then looked at me and asked, "Don't I know you from somewhere?"

I replied, "Maybe you do."

She then went to visit a friend of hers who worked in the jewelry store located in the hotel lobby. I sent a waiter from one of the restaurants to go to the lady and ask her to come back, because I wanted to talk to her. She came back, and we talked about fifteen or twenty minutes.

After a while, she asked me, "When do you get off work? Do you want to come over to my place?"

"Most definitely," I replied, with my imagination running wild.

After work I made myself a large "to go" drink of Southern Comfort. Happy about the night ahead, I headed to her place. Once I arrived she invited me in.

"Would you like a cup of coffee?" she asked.

I said, "No, I brought my own drink."

She asked me to have a seat on the couch. We talked for a little bit, and then she looked right into my eyes and asked me, "Do you know why I invited you here?"

"I think so," I replied with anticipation.

Then she said, "I invited you because I wanted to tell you that Jesus loves you and cares about your life."

That was not what I was expecting.

"On second thought," I replied, "I'll take that cup of coffee."

The truth was I had just been set up by God. That night changed my life. I stayed and talked with her until four o'clock in the morning. I even went back the next night to talk some more. She and her friends took me to church two nights later where I had an encounter with Jesus. My life was forever changed because that young lady reached out to me and spoke these eight powerful words to me: "Jesus loves you and cares about your life." Thank God that in all my nights of drinking and drugs, I never died in a car accident and stepped into eternity, lost before I could hear and respond to those words.

A few days later I went into a Christian bookstore looking to buy my first Bible and some new music. One of the guys with whom I had gone to college was in the store.

"Paul, what are you doing in here?" he asked.

"I'm looking for music," I answered.

"But this is a Christian bookstore," he said.

"I know."

"So why are you here?"

"I'm looking for music."

"But the only kind of music here is Christian music."

"Yes, I know. I'm looking for Christian music."

"But only Christians listen to Christian music."

"I know. I'm a Christian."

"No, you're not."

"Yes, I am."

"No, you're not. I was in class with you for three months. I know you're not a Christian."

"Yes, I am. Three days ago I gave my life to Jesus. I was saved and filled with the Holy Spirit!"

He looked at me and began to weep. Then he hugged me, and I thought, "Christians are weird folks!"

After he stopped crying, I was able to get him off of me. My shirt was wet with his tears. Then he said to me, "I am so sorry. I am so sorry."

"What are you so sorry about?" I asked him.

"Three times a week when you would come into class, the Lord would tell me, 'Talk to him, talk to him. Tell him, "Jesus loves you and cares about your life."'"

Eight words!

"I can't do that," he would say to God. "No way can I do that! He's impossible. He might hit me or cuss me out."

The reason he reacted that way was because I would come to class drunk or stoned. Our class was a speech class, and my speeches were very carnal and off the wall. He had no idea how hurt and lost I was, and that is why he had argued with God.

But he was wrong and so are we if we think that we cannot reach out to others who are in need just as I was at that time in my life. I was not impossible to reach; no one is! All it takes is a willing heart to reach out and speak those eight words, especially when you have the leading of God to speak to someone. Whom has Jesus placed in your life so you can speak those eight words to them?

Let me interject this: I do not believe it is the wisdom of God to invite an unsaved, half-drunk individual to your house after midnight to tell them Jesus loves them. I am not suggesting that to anyone. That is just how it happened with me. But I will say this: that lady is a dear friend to this day, and she did one more wonderful thing. She introduced me to her friends, one of whom is Shoddy, who became my wife. Through this bold, loving, and obedient lady, I was introduced to two of the greatest gifts in my life: Jesus Christ and my wife.

He Spoke Eight Words Too

Now the word of the LORD came to Jonah the second time, saying, "Arise, go to Nineveh, that great city, and preach to it the message that I tell you." So Jonah arose and went to Nineveh, according to the word of the LORD. Now Nineveh was an exceedingly great city, a three-day journey in extent. And Jonah began to enter the city on the first day's walk. Then he cried out, and said, "Yet forty days, and Nineveh shall be overthrown!"

—JONAH 3:1–4

Note the end of this passage. It says, *Yet forty days, and Nineveh shall be overthrown!* These eight powerful words would cause a nation to repent and turn toward God. But Jonah needed a change of heart to become willing to speak these words, because he had a judgmental attitude toward the people whom God was seeking to save.

Jonah was one of the prophets of Israel and lived during the time of the great Assyrian Empire with Nineveh as its capital city. (Today, Nineveh is located in northern Iraq in the land of the Kurds.) Jonah had just one problem: he had no love for Nineveh! Nineveh was the long-standing enemy of Israel, and the Ninevites were a notoriously cruel people. They were responsible for spreading death, suffering, and destruction wherever they went, specifically among the Jewish people. So Jonah had a serious problem. God had given him a word that he did not want to deliver, even though it meant salvation for an entire city.

We know the story: Jonah decided to run from God. As we all are aware, running from God never works out very well. By running away, Jonah was saying to God, "I do not want to do that. I do not want to get involved in the lives of those people in that wicked city. They deserve to die. They are mean, cruel, and nasty. I do not care anything about them."

Jonah fled on a ship that was traveling six hundred miles in the wrong direction. While on that ship, a great storm arose and rocked it. We are told that Jonah had gone down into the lowest part of the ship, had lain down and fallen fast asleep.

The captain went to him and said, *What do you mean, sleeper? Arise, call on your God; perhaps your God will consider us, so that we may not perish* (Jon. 1:6). The captain was pleading with Jonah to wake up, rise up, and do something. It is a sad day when the world has to wake us up and plead with us to call on our God because everything they have done has failed.

After getting tossed overboard by the sailors, being swallowed by a great fish, and finally being regurgitated back onto dry land, the reluctant prophet finally obeyed, entered the city, and delivered his eight words from God. That was all he said, but God took those eight words and used them to turn the hearts of the people of Nineveh. As a result, the entire city repented.

You may not be a prophet like Jonah who was called to speak to a city or nation, but certainly you have dealt with some similar challenges, like wanting people to get what they deserve. The Assyrians were cruel, barbaric people who had brought tremendous suffering and pain to the Jews. Jonah revealed the conflict of his heart when he acknowledged God's ways, which were in contrast to how he felt toward the Ninevites. In essence, Jonah told God, *I fled... [because] I know you are a gracious and merciful God, slow to anger and abundant in lovingkindness, One who relents from doing harm* (Jon. 4:2). Jonah was aware of the grace and mercies of God that would touch the Ninevites. He did not doubt what God could or would do. His struggle was with understanding how God could extend this love, mercy, and forgiveness to such undeserving people.

All God asked from Jonah was to deliver eight words to the ears of the Ninevites; God would touch their hearts and do the rest. Will you and I allow the compassion of God to take hold of us and flow through our lives? Or will we struggle with a judgment, an offense, or simple reluctance to go because we do not yet grasp how the grace and mercy of God should flow so freely into another person's life?

There may be eight words you could speak that would release people from a crushing weight of regret or pain they carry, words such as, "I forgive you for what you have done." Your words can open the door so that repentance—a changing of direction for someone's life—can begin. Let us always remember: it is the goodness of God that leads people to repentance, and mercy triumphs over judgment. (See Romans 2:4; James 2:13.)

It took being swallowed by the great fish and living in its belly for three days for Jonah to become willing to step into people's lives. Even when God saved the whole city, Jonah was not very happy. He wanted God to judge the Ninevites, not to save them. Sometimes we may struggle with those same thoughts and attitudes.

Considering the story of Jonah, we see how the captain, the sailors, the wind, the sea, the great fish, the king, the Ninevites, the sun, the plant, and even the worm obeyed God. (If you are unfamiliar with the worm and the plant, I encourage you to read the entire story.) But Jonah, on the other hand, only obeyed to speak on God's behalf after much reluctance. Jonah seriously needed to take hold of God's values. I find it interesting that Jonah is the only book in the Bible that ends with a question about having compassion: *Should I not have compassion on Nineveh, the great city in which there are more than*

120,000 persons who do not know the difference between their right and left hand, as well as many animals? (Jon. 4:11, NAS).

Are we willing to allow God's love message to the world to be a greater factor in our actions than our fears, our judgments, or opinions? What will it take to jerk us out of our seats of security to go and speak to those whom God cares about? Hopefully, it will not take a whale, just a willing heart and a sincere *yes* to God.

CHAPTER 3

COMPASSION VERSUS SYMPATHY

[The LORD's] compassions fail not.

—LAMENTATIONS 3:22

When you say yes to God, you will be surprised by the doors that will swing open for you to demonstrate a heart of compassion. Sometimes the only thing people need is a simple touch, a listening ear, or a few kind words. A willing heart—along with an attentive ear, gracious words, and a kind hand—can bring the touch of heaven into a person's life. We might not genuinely feel everyone's pain as they do, but we can be involved in rescuing those who cross our paths.

Jesus did not come just to feel pain and suffering, sorrow and misery. His feelings motivated Him to action. Compassion *moved* Him. This is why He let people touch Him. He knew that when they touched Him and He felt their suffering, love would flow and lives would be changed.

Do not let any internal obstacle keep you from moving in the direction to meet a need. Rise above the fear of failure, the shackles of shame, the distress of disappointment, and the pride of prejudice. Satan uses mental images, thoughts, and words to prevent us from being instruments of God's love, because he knows that once compassion begins to flow, life-changing results always follow.

Sympathy and Compassion

The author of Hebrews wrote regarding Jesus, *For we have not a high priest which cannot be touched with the feeling of our infirmities* (Heb. 4:15, KJV). This brings us to the subject of sympathy and compassion. The first thing to note is that sympathy and compassion are different. They are, however, related; and they have a cousin called empathy.

Sympathy feels for other people and acknowledges their pain. It is the act or capacity of entering into the feelings or interests of another. When we operate in sympathy, we are concerned for a person's well-being and try to identify with their heartaches without having personally felt their pain. *Empathy*, on the other hand, identifies with those with whom we share a common experience. We feel their pain because we have lived it somewhere in our past. Finally, *compassion* is a result of sympathy and empathy. When acted upon, compassion motivates us to work to alleviate that which brings suffering to others.

Both sympathy and empathy are important because they allow us to open our hearts to others. But we do not want to get stuck on a feeling! It is not God's intention for us to just go around and feel others' pain. How horrible would that be, and what purpose would it serve? Neither sympathy nor empathy should be the end of our response to others; they should be the gateway to compassion, which results in acts of mercy, grace, and demonstrations of God's love through us to them.

Sympathy has no hands. Sympathy feels bad for a person when he or she has no food for his or her family. Compassion takes the person to the grocery store and stocks the empty pantry with food. Sympathy feels, but compassionate lovingkindness looks for ways to manifest those feelings in practical ways. You can know you are walking in compassion and not just sympathy when you see a problem or someone in pain, you allow it to touch you on the inside, and then you are motivated to try to bring about a change in that situation. *Compassion is the hands of Jesus.*

At one time or another, we have all felt sympathy for someone's pain. We have shared another's feelings, but that person was still grieved, sick, broke, hurting, or confused. We want to share their feelings and try to comfort them; but after a while, those people do not want us just to understand their feelings. They are desperate for us to help *change* their situation.

Compassion is a compelling, strong desire to change what is felt. Caring people not only *feel* another's pain and suffering, they also *act* to lessen the load and to ease the discomfort. Compassion allows a situation to touch our hearts in such a way that we cannot leave the situation in the same condition in which we found it. Only the love and grace of God in us give us the ability to feel people's pains and sorrows and then move us to change them. It is important to note that God's intention is that we not become drained in the process. They key is to remember that *God* is the source of all answers and help. We are simply conduits, channels through whom He can flow.

Every time we see Jesus confronted by a tragic situation, He immediately was moved to do something to reverse the conditions of those who suffered. The love and compassion of the Father were compelling forces in His life that propelled Him to minister to the deaf, the leper, the one caught in sin, and the cripple. To each of their lives, Jesus brought change.

Sometimes we reach a point where we no longer want to feel other people's pain. We want to have a happy life. Sometimes we just do not want to be bothered, especially at those times when we feel consumed with our own issues. We do not want to feel misery and suffering all the time with no relief or solution. Who does? We have to do more than just be a dumping ground for people's problems. If not, pretty soon we will end up walking through life looking as bad as they do—sad, heavy, and weighed down with the woes of the world. We start with listening and feeling, but we have to go to the next level where we put motion into our emotion as we work together with people to find ways to heal their pain, overcome their negativity, and help them bring resolution to their predicaments. People need a touch from Jesus; and as His body, our hands are His hands.

When we come across people in great distress, we need to reach out and relate to them. We listen. We feel. We sympathize. That is good; in fact, it is scriptural. In Romans 12:15, Paul tells us, *Rejoice with them that do rejoice, and weep with them that weep* (KJV). But as good as that is, it is only the beginning. As a community of believers, as Christians, we are to feel others' pain, hurt, sadness, poverty, and lack. Once we feel their pain, however, we must move into compassionate action. We generate change by imparting the power of God into their lives.

Love Overcomes the Shame Factor

But what does it say? "The word is near you, in your mouth and in your heart" (that is, the word of faith which we preach): that if you confess with your mouth the Lord Jesus and believe in your heart that God has raised Him from the dead, you will be saved. For with the heart one believes unto righteousness, and with the mouth confession is made unto salvation. For the Scripture says, "Whoever believes on Him will not be put to shame."

—ROMANS 10:8–11

Shame is the plague of our day. In Asia, where I live and minister, the shame factor is much greater than it is in most other regions of the world. Unfortunately, it is also strong among many Christians. Guilt is the feeling we have concerning what we have *done*, whereas shame is the feeling we have about who we *are*. Both leave us incapacitated and isolated. The effects of shame can be internal and external. Internally, shame is reflected in a negative view of ourselves based upon real or imagined circumstances. Toxic shame creates insecurity and self-condemnation, making us unable to view ourselves as God does. It hinders the free flow of love for others because it is so blinded by its own needs. Shame is a blinding factor that hinders us from seeing others with our spiritual eyes.

External shame can be manifested as embarrassment—producing insecurity about our beliefs—or a judgmental spirit where we judge others as we judge ourselves. The sense of shame destroys the genuine you, resulting in the loss of self-esteem and manifesting in depression, rage, anger, and control. This shame keeps us from living the abundant life Jesus came to give us and hinders us from stepping out in faith to help anyone else. When we are overly concerned about what people will think of us and afraid of what they might say, we are going to be embarrassed and ashamed if we fail. This self-focus generated by fear will cause us to constantly look at ourselves, and we will not be able to see others.

In Romans 1:16, Paul declared, *For I am not ashamed of the gospel of Christ, for it is the power of God to salvation for everyone who believes, for the Jew first and also for the Greek.* What Paul meant was, "I am not afraid of proclaiming the gospel to others because I know it will not let me down. In spite of my weakness, I am more convinced of the power of God than I am of my own fears. I am not afraid. I am not overly conscious of myself when I reach out to others with lovingkindness. I am not afraid that I am going to look like a fool or that God might abandon me and leave me there all alone. I have great confidence in God and His grace working in me. God's power overcomes my shame and weakness."

The gospel is the power of God to those who believe. So in order for them to receive the power of God, they have to have something to believe. They must hear it first, because how can they believe what they have never heard?

In verse 11 of Romans 10, Paul said, *whoever believes on Him will not be put to shame.*

When we give people the message, the gospel, that good news will be accompanied with all the power of God to change their lives. We must be free from shame to deliver that word with grace and courage, knowing we will see God's Word prevail.

The gospel is not the message of man. It is the good news of heaven. It is the plan of God. It is a powerful declaration of the will and the purpose of God. If we truly believe, we will have no shame, no disgrace when we approach people with the Word. We can have confidence that the very God who spoke those words will back them up with His power.

Rich God, Poor God

*For there is no distinction between Jew and Greek, for **the same Lord over all is rich to all who call upon Him.** For "whoever calls upon the name of the* LORD *shall be saved"* (Rom. 10:12–13, emphasis added).

Your vision of God will determine how you reflect Him to others. If you have a poor image of God—that He is vengeful, uncaring, and unloving—then that vision will control you and affect how you reflect Him to people. This problem has crippled many today. Their view of God has been corrupted through painful experiences with negative church people or by certain messages that have been legalistic and condemning. We cannot allow how we see God to be determined by what men say or do. Our view of Him must be determined by what He reveals about Himself in His Word and not by the opinions of others based upon their experiences.

Sadly, those who represent God have not always done a great job. People have been disappointed and wounded because someone misrepresented God to them. As a result, these people carry a lasting negative impression. Unfortunately, there has been more legalism than love, more rejection than reaching, and more criticism than caring in some people's lives. But it was a *person* who created this scenario of pain; it was not *Jesus*. Jesus has never walked out on, abandoned, used, or taken advantage of anyone. One of the sad commentaries of our times is that God has been recreated into the image that misguided people have of Him. This is a poor God image that does not resemble the truth.

Paul asserts that God is *rich* to all those that call upon Him. God's bank is filled with the riches of love, forgiveness, kindness, grace, and mercy. We have access to what He has made available to us, and we need to tell others of this life-changing news.

If a man has AIDS, he does not need a million dollars; he needs the healing power of God. If a woman is demon-possessed, she does not need a new car; she needs someone to come in the name of Jesus and break the power of the devil over her life and deliver her. But how can anyone receive what he or she really needs if the person does not know that it is available to him or her? Even if the individual does gain that knowledge, how can he or she receive God's gifts if the person believes that he or she is ineligible to receive them?

We must counter all the misinformation out there about God and let people know how rich our God is and how He wants to bless them. The apostle Paul said it this way: *Now all things are of God, who has reconciled us to Himself through Jesus Christ, and has given us the ministry of reconciliation, that is, that God was in Christ reconciling the world to Himself, not imputing their trespasses to them, and has committed to us the word of reconciliation* (2 Cor. 5:18–19).

God is not angry with people, holding their sin against them. How wonderful and liberating it is to be able to tell people how loved they are and not how bad they have been! God is rich to those who call upon Him. But if people do not understand how rich He is, they will never avail themselves of His great blessings. In order to receive His goodness in their lives, people must understand that

He wants to make it available to them—not because they deserve it, nor because they can earn it, but because it is in His character to do so because He loves them. This is all possible because Jesus paid for it with His blood. They have to know that if they will believe, God will release His blessing upon them. If they do not know that, they will not call upon Him. And if they do not call upon Him, then that richness of God—whether it is provision, forgiveness, healing, deliverance, or anything else they need—will not be released.

The first act of compassionate love we can display to the world is to tell people that forgiveness is paid for by the blood of Jesus and the goodness of God is freely available to them. It does not matter about their background, ethnicity, education, or social status. None of those things matter to God! What matters to Him is that we believe and receive the blood of Jesus that was shed to purchase all the good things that God wants to pour out upon us. It is not about our goodness; it is about His grace.

How Can They Believe Without a Preacher?

The riches of God's mercy and grace are available to anyone who will believe and receive. They receive by calling upon Him, but how can they believe and receive without a preacher? Paul understood this dilemma when he wrote, *How then shall they call on Him in whom they have not believed? And how shall they believe in Him of who they have not heard? And how shall they hear without a preacher?* (Rom. 10:14).

People are not going to call on someone they do not believe in. They are not going to believe in someone they have never heard about. How can they hear about that someone without a preacher to come and tell them?

You may say, "What you are saying is true, but I am not a preacher." In one sense, you are a preacher; all of us are ministers of the gospel. The only difference is the platform from which we speak. Remember, we all have the ministry of reconciliation. Some are specifically called to preach behind a pulpit, but *all* are called to be preachers or communicators outside the church. Every one of us has our own platform in everyday life. One of the greatest tools of the believer today is lifestyle evangelism. All of us have the responsibility to minister to people with whom we come in contact. I believe people long to see the reality of Jesus lived out in daily life where everyone faces challenges and complications.

By sharing without shame, giving with generosity, and touching with tenderness, we live out the life and love of God. We demonstrate the good news and let people know the difference it can make in their lives. Compassion compels us. Love empowers us. His Son indwells us. We are God's plan to touch the world; together, we are the church.

One of the members of our church in the Philippines is a businessman named Peter. This man took a mission trip to China. He had not prepared ahead of time what he would say or do, but God told him to go, and he went, accompanied by some other Christian brothers. When Peter arrived in China, he realized that there were some things God wanted him to speak to the people, but he was nervous about what he would say. Then he remembered a passage in the Old Testament in which Jeremiah expressed his inability to speak for the Lord:

Then the word of the LORD came to me, saying: "Before I formed you in the womb I knew you; before you were born I sanctified you; I ordained you a prophet to the nations."

Then said I: "Ah, Lord GOD! Behold, I cannot speak, for I am a youth."

But the LORD said to me: "Do not say, 'I am a youth,' For you shall go to all to whom I send you, and whatever I command you, you shall speak."

"Do not be afraid of their faces, for I am with you to deliver you," says the LORD.

Then the LORD put forth His hand and touched my mouth, and the LORD said to me: "Behold, I have put My words in your mouth."

—JEREMIAH 1:4–9

Acting on that passage, my friend Peter found himself preaching and sharing for hours, laying hands on people, breaking the power of the devil, and seeing freedom come into people's lives. He is not a preacher; he is a businessman, but that day he was a powerful vessel of the good news. Peter made himself available, and God's grace was his ability. You do not have to be in China for that to happen. Your willingness and availability combined with the grace of God in you are always a winning combination, whoever you are and wherever you may be.

The people with whom you come into contact in your everyday life do not need a pastor as much as they need a friend—someone who knows the truth and will share with them the good news accompanied with God's power. Their lives may stink. They may be hurting. They may be wounded physically, mentally or emotionally, but you have a message that can bring them healing from the Lord.

They may be sitting beside you in church, in school, or at work. You are God's loving gift to them to bring healing and help.

Paul said that the gospel is the power of God to those who believe. We are "those who believe." Now we have to believe that this message, this Word, this good news, is the power of God to bring change to people's lives. Once we start to really believe, God's loving passion for others will become a reality in their lives through us.

It is not our job to convince people to believe in us. We are not trying to sell ourselves. We are not trying to preach ourselves. We are not going to answer their prayers or fix their problems. *The Lord* is the One who is going to do that. We are not their savior. We are not their healer. We are not their deliverer. We are merely the people who point the way to the One who is Savior, healer, and deliverer, and His name is Jesus.

If we are going to be any help to anyone, we have to *wake up*, step outside our comfort zones, extend ourselves despite our insecurities, and let go of our fears of failure. I promise you, once you have experienced being His vessel, His compassion will change you. You will live each day looking for what God sees and expecting to be used by Him. You will live differently, and, as a result, so will all those whom you meet. God wants to ignite a passion within each of us. Zeal, excitement, and joy will stir up the power He has deposited within us. Once released, it will flow freely and unhindered from us. Our world is waiting for us to release the compassion of God! Your world is waiting for you!

CHAPTER 4

YOU HAVE YOUR FATHER'S EYES

That which was from the beginning, which we have heard, which we have seen with our eyes, which we have looked upon, and our hands have handled, concerning the Word of life—the life was manifested, and we have seen, and bear witness, and declare unto you.

—1 John 1:1–2

In the beginning, God created man in His image. God is a tripartite being—a trinity, three united as one. He is Father, Son, and Holy Spirit. Man is also a tripartite being. Man is a spirit, he has a soul, and he lives in a body. It is in the spirit where we are made in the likeness of God.

In Genesis, God breathed into man the breath—or the spirit of—life. Through our spirit we communicate with God, receive revelation from Him, and worship Him. By the Spirit in our spirits, we become God-conscious. The soul is our interior being where we are self-conscious. The soul is composed of mind, will, and emotions. It is through the soul that our personalities are revealed. The body is made of this earth, giving us the ability to be physically aware and involved. It is through our bodies that we come into contact with our physical world and with those around us. Our bodies are endowed with five senses: seeing, hearing, touching, smelling, and tasting. It is through these that we experience the pleasures, and sometimes pains, in this physical world.

The light bulb is a good object to illustrate the functions of spirit, soul, and body. The spirit is the electricity, the ultimate source of all light. The soul is the wire, the delivery system of electricity. The body is the glass bulb where the manifestation of the electricity is delivered by the wire. Jesus said that we are the light of the world. (See Matthew 5:14.)

It is through the five senses that we feel and communicate with the world around us. John declared that the spiritual things the disciples had heard, seen, and touched were the foundations for the words they declared. Our Christianity brings Jesus to people where they can hear from us, receive a touch from us, and experience change as a result of Jesus being made real in a tangible way through us. It is when we allow all three parts of ourselves to work in unity that the life of God we carry is shared effectively. We have a mind that yields to the leading of the Spirit and a body that is submitted to serve and become a vessel of help and healing. It delivers a touch of strength and words of life. Our lives reflect Him when all three parts are working in unity.

And when He came near the gate of the city, behold, a dead man was being carried out, the only son of his mother; and she was a widow. And a large crowd from the city was with her.

When the Lord saw her, He had compassion on her and said to her, "Do not weep."

Then He came and touched the open coffin, and those who carried him stood still. And He said, "Young man, I say to you, arise."

So he who was dead sat up and began to speak. And he presented him to his mother.

—LUKE 7:12–15

In these verses we see a captivating progression of sight, touch, and speech: the Lord saw the woman, He came to her and touched her, then He spoke words to her. Seeing a mother weeping over the death of her son prompted Jesus to reach out and touch. Jesus touched the coffin, and then He spoke. The life and love within Him were released through His words and His touch.

Compassion is not compassion until it is manifested through the actions prompted by our senses. It is the God-created way in which we express the love of God toward others. God has given us eyes to see, ears to hear, hands to touch, and a voice to speak His Word into the lives of the hurting people all around us.

True Judgments

The Spirit of the LORD shall rest upon Him, the Spirit of wisdom and understanding, the Spirit of counsel and might, the Spirit of knowledge and of the fear of the LORD. His delight is in the fear of the LORD, and **He shall not judge by the sight of His eyes, nor decide by the hearing of His ears** (ISA. 11:1–3, emphasis added).

In the emphasized portion of these verses, the prophet Isaiah was not discounting the value of our senses in communicating with the world. Instead, he was pointing out how the Lord processes information. The Lord allows His seeing and hearing to transcend the physical senses, and we are to follow His example. As our bodies speak to us through what they sense and our minds bring forth reasoning, it is important that these things do not overshadow our spirits as our primary source of perception.

In John 5:30, Jesus said, *I can of Myself do nothing. As I hear, I judge; and My judgment is righteous, because I do not seek My own will but the will of the Father who sent Me.*

In other words, the true judgments we make in life cannot be based solely upon physical senses. Many times our senses do not communicate the whole story. Sometimes there is more to a situation than meets the eye. There are conditions that are not so obvious. That is why people manipulate physical circumstances to deceive. They will portray something very different than the hidden agendas or motives in their hearts. But when we have inner discernment by the Holy Spirit complementing our physical senses, our ability to make decisions and take action to meet the immediate needs around us will be more effective. When we have a knowing, a seeing, and a hearing that come from within our spirits, we can make judgments that do more than apply salve to the immediate need. We will be able to discern root issues and help deliver more long-term solutions for people's lives. Remember, we are spirit beings living inside earthly bodies.

Many people have become great actors and put on convincing performances. While some come across very hard and rough, they actually could be trying to protect a wounded heart. The reason they are so hard and angry is because they are working desperately to protect themselves from ever being hurt again. They are the walking wounded. If I only look with my eyes and only listen with my ears, what I will see is this very hard, angry person. But when I have *discerning eyes*, illuminated by the Spirit of God within me, I can see someone who is hurt, wounded, and in tremendous need— ready to crumble at any moment. *Hearing from our hearts* gives us the ability to respond in a more beneficial way to what we hear with our physical ears. Therefore, we need to engage our spiritual senses, which will protect and provide strength for our physical senses.

The Light of the Body Is the Eye

Sight is the ability of the eye to focus on its surroundings and to detect images. Physiologists tell us that all objects are illuminated with light. When we look at people, what we see is the light of illumination traveling off of them toward us and that light is picked up by the lens of the eye. The lens then transmits that image to the retina. The retina takes a snapshot of that image by use of the cells that have the ability to focus and to distinguish colors. The snapshot gathered by the retina is then transmitted to the brain for final processing. The mind—which is part of the soul, as we have said— then makes decisions on what is done with that information.

Here is a powerful truth: *without light there can be no sight*. If our souls are damaged, that light is negatively processed through eyes of lust, greed, jealousy, anger, and judgment. However, if our souls are healthy and renewed, the light is processed in a positive way so that it sees with pure and compassionate eyes. Concerning the issue of the eye, Jesus said, *The lamp of the body is the eye. Therefore, when your eye is good, your whole body also is full of light. But when your eye is bad, your body also is full of darkness* (Luke 11:34).

Blindness is caused either by an injury or a disease whereby a person loses his or her visual perception. Blindness is caused when the lens is either clouded over, like in the case of cataracts, or when the retina is damaged and can no longer process images due to its lost ability to transmit those images to the brain. Paul, in writing to the church at Corinth, declared this spiritual truth: *Whose minds the god of this age has blinded, who do not believe, lest the light of the gospel of the glory of Christ, who is the image of God, should shine on them* (2 Cor. 4:4).

Our job as followers of Jesus is to declare the gospel in such a way that the light of God can remove the blindness that is in the minds and hearts of people. This gospel is the power of God. When proclaimed by passionate and compassionate men and women, the gospel will reverse the curse of darkness and cause the hearer to be able to see the glory of God revealed in the face of Christ.

The Eyes of Jesus

But Jesus turned around, and when He saw her He said, 'Be of good cheer, daughter; your faith has made you well.' And the woman was made well from that hour.... But when He saw the multitudes, He was moved with compassion for them, because they were weary and scattered, like sheep having no shepherd (Matt. 9:22, 36).

And when Jesus went out He saw a great multitude; and He was moved with compassion for them, and healed their sick (Matt. 14:14).

When Jesus saw their faith, He said to the paralytic, "Son, your sins are forgiven you" (Mark 2:5).

And Jesus, when he came out, saw a great multitude and was moved with compassion for them, because they were like sheep not having a shepherd. So He began to teach them many things (Mark 6:34).

But when Jesus saw her, He called her to Him and said to her, "Woman, you are loosed from your infirmity" (Luke 13:12).

When Jesus had raised Himself up and saw no one but the woman, He said to her, "Woman, where are those accusers of yours? Has no one condemned you?" She said, "No one, Lord." And Jesus said to her, "Neither do I condemn you; go and sin no more" (John 8:10–11).

Therefore, when Jesus saw her weeping, and the Jews who came with her weeping, He groaned in the spirit and was troubled. And He said, "Where have you laid him?" They said to Him, "Lord, come and see." Jesus wept (John 11:33–35).

Jesus's perceptions were developed by the times He spent in His Father's presence. He had developed this discipline from the time He was twelve years old, where it was said He increased in wisdom and stature and in favor with God. This practice continued to His time in the desert and on the mountain. This time He had with His Father enabled Jesus to become adept at seeing through His Father's eyes. In John 5:19, Jesus put it this way: *"Most assuredly, I say to you, the Son can do nothing of Himself, but what He sees the Father do; for whatever He does, the Son also does."*

Jesus saw what His Father saw, and then He did what His Father would have Him to do! When Jesus "saw," it meant more than a glance; it meant He truly considered, perceived, became aware of, and had true knowledge of situations He came to change. Every time Jesus saw the needs of those around Him, compassion aroused Him, moving Him to take action. Those who were blind, deaf, demon-possessed, in sin, and even the dead were changed by the miraculous power of God when Jesus was moved by and released compassion. The anointing within Him was activated by the eyes of love that truly saw the need and not merely the symptom.

The Bible says that when Jesus saw the throngs, He was moved with compassion for them because they were bewildered, harassed, distressed, dejected, and helpless. His eyes were attracted to those living on the outer fringes of Jewish society, who were disinherited, dispossessed, and depressed. Jesus looked into their eyes and saw the tragedy that engulfed them. He saw people who were ready to give up and quit. But He moved in sync with heaven's purpose and the compassionate love He had in His heart for them. These were the forces that compelled Him. His was an example of the light of God's love invading the darkest bondages in people's lives.

The Story of a Good Samaritan

And behold, a certain lawyer stood up and tested Him, saying, "Teacher, what shall I do to inherit eternal life?"

He said to him, "What is written in the law? What is your reading of it?"

So he answered and said, "You shall love the LORD your God with all your heart, with all your soul, with all your strength, and with all your mind," and "your neighbor as yourself."

And he said to him "You have answered rightly; do this and you will live."

But he, wanting to justify himself, said to Jesus, "And who is my neighbor?"

Then Jesus answered and said: "A certain man went down from Jerusalem to Jericho, and fell among thieves, who stripped him of his clothing, wounded him, and departed, leaving him half dead.

"Now by chance a certain priest came down that road. And when he saw him, he passed by on the other side.

"Likewise a Levite, when he arrived at the place, came and looked, and passed by on the other side.

"But a certain Samaritan, as he journeyed, came where he was. And when he saw him, he had compassion. So he went to him and bandaged his wounds, pouring on oil and wine; and he set him on his own animal, brought him to an inn, and took care of him.

"On the next day, when he departed, he took out two denarii, gave them to the innkeeper, and said to him, 'Take care of him; and whatever more you spend, when I come again, I will repay you.'"

—LUKE 10:25–35

The context of this story is a dialogue that occurred between Jesus and a Jewish lawyer. The lawyers in those days were actually scribes whose function was to write down and teach the laws of Moses. In addition, they also rendered rulings to settle disputes concerning the law.

In answer to the lawyer's question, "What is the greatest commandment?" Jesus responded with what became known as the Great Commandment: *You shall love the LORD your God with all your heart, with all your soul, and with all your mind...and...your neighbor as yourself* (Matt. 22:37–39). Or, as we say at our church, New Life, "Love God wholeheartedly and love people fervently."

As if Jesus were on the witness stand, the lawyer fired back with another question. "Who is my neighbor?"

In response to this query, Jesus said, "Let me tell you a story..."

The story began with a man leaving Jerusalem and headed for Jericho. The Jericho road was treacherous. On it, many innocent victims had fallen prey to bandits. It was a winding, meandering road, conducive for ambushing. The road from Jerusalem to Jericho is seventeen miles long and drops about three thousand feet within those seventeen miles. That is one dangerous road. In the days of Jesus, it came to be known as the "Bloody Pass."[1]

This parable tells us that a certain man started out from Jerusalem down the Bloody Pass. On the way, he was confronted by a band of thieves who stripped him of all his clothing and beat him, almost to the point of death. After a while, a priest passed by and *saw* the man lying in the ditch but quickly moved over to the other side of the road and continued his journey. Later, a Levite (Levites were the assistants to the priests) passed by, *looked* at the man, be he also kept going.

These two men represent all that is wrong with religion, which causes us to be self-righteous, critical, judgmental, and uncaring. I can almost hear them speaking. "Well, I wonder what this man did to bring all this trouble on himself. I cannot defile myself by dealing with him. He should not have been traveling alone anyway. I am sure it must have been his fault. He probably got what he deserved. If he had been living right, this would not have happened to him."

They looked at the man's situation but they did not really see him. They did not have the Father's eyes, because they did not have the Father's heart. They were more concerned about getting to Jerusalem to get on with their own religious duties than in taking care of a person in great need. For all the priest knew, the man was dead. This meant that if he had stopped and gone near, he would have been defiled. And if defiled, he would have been required to go through a ceremonial washing and a restoring of ritual purity, which would be time consuming and costly. In the meantime, he would not have been able to collect, distribute, or partake of tithes. In other words, the price of helping this wounded man would have been too costly to the priest; therefore, he chose to look away and keep moving. In contrast, God's people, who allow His love to flow through their hearts, are not afraid to get dirty, to touch those in need, or to reach out and help people in horrible situations.

Finally, a Samaritan passed by that wounded man. Samaritans, according to history, were descendants of the tribes of Ephraim and Manasseh, part of the northern tribes of Israel. Their temple of worship was at Mount Gerizim, which they believed was the original location of the Holy Place. They considered themselves to be the true keepers of the law. Historically, great animosity existed between the northern and southern Jewish kingdoms until the time of Jesus. The Jews accused the Samaritans of blasphemy and were offended by their forms of worship and religious practices, even though they were quite similar to their own. The religious and ethnic prejudices between these two groups manifested in their refusal to have anything to do with each other.

You would not expect a Samaritan to be the hero of this story, but he was. When he *saw* this tragic situation, he was moved with compassion. Compassion will make us stop in our tracks when we see people in need. Compassion stops us but also causes us to respond. Love will not let us look away and do nothing. When we see with eyes of mercy, our hands will be quick to take action. When we see as Jesus sees and allow situations to touch our hearts, we will act as Jesus acts. The religious leaders in this parable were blinded by their own self-importance and religious attitudes, but this was not true of the Samaritan. All he saw was another human being in need of help. How could he not respond?

We call this the parable of the Good Samaritan, but it is also a story about who Jesus is and who we are supposed to be. This man did not have the dreaded Christian neck disease, which I call the "look-aways," which manifests as "Do not look. Do not get involved. It is not my responsibility."

Well, if it is not our responsibility, then whose is it? Our responsibility is to simply respond with the ability that we carry. We have the Father's heart and eyes, so we are to be moved by compassion to take action in love by putting ourselves on the line for others.

In this parable, Jesus taught the lawyer about the way of salvation, loving God, and loving his neighbor. It is a story about love being an action, not a religious idea. Compassion is something you feel and do. This man on the roadside could be any person. Jesus is teaching us who our neighbor is: our neighbor is anyone we happen to encounter in life, no matter who they are.

People who are not saved are half dead; they are alive on the outside but dead on the inside. Jesus is like the Samaritan who comes by, sees the wounded, and stops. He pours in the oil and the wine—the new birth and the Holy Spirit. He then takes them to the innkeeper. What is the inn? That is the church. There, Jesus commits them to the care of His people who continue to minister to their needs through the power of the indwelling Holy Spirit. Just like the Samaritan, Jesus pays for everything and promises to return.

Jesus is the One who found us robbed, wounded by the enemy, and half dead. Jesus had compassion on us, just as this Samaritan had compassion on the wounded man beside the road. Do you realize that you and I are also the good Samaritans of life? Like the Samaritan in the story, we, too, are traveling down life's road when, all of a sudden, we encounter situations like the half-beaten man in the ditch who really needs our help. This incident with the wounded man was not something the Samaritan had on his schedule for the day; it was something that just happened. But that did not keep him from stopping and doing what he could do to help. He made himself available and took time to express God's merciful love. He was prepared to respond to a supposed "interruption" in the course of his day.

Have you ever realized that very few of the miracles that Jesus performed were scheduled events? Most were simply interruptions. People had not called His secretary to set up an appointment asking Him to come and do a miracle, feed hungry people, or heal a few folks. Jesus's ministry was performed day by day along the way as He went into one town and after another. Interruptions became divine appointments.

As we live our daily lives, we must be available to make a difference. Ministry to others is not something reserved for Sunday morning or Sunday night or just inside the church walls. It is a lifestyle that we are supposed to live out Monday through Sunday. Even the Samaritan found the one in need *outside* the walls of worship. Wherever we are, coming or going, we have what the wounded, naked, half-dead people out there desperately need. And the only way it is going to reach them is for us to see their needs, allow grace to take hold of us, and let compassion motivate us to go to them and pour into their lives.

What are we to do when a "God opportunity" presents itself to us? We are to stop, look, and listen for the Holy Spirit to show us what to do. We have eyes that others do not have—we have the Father's eyes. We have a heart of compassion that others do not possess. When we see a wounded heart, we know that God wants us to step into the situation because we carry His love answer to the world.

An Opportunity to Practice What I Am Preaching

I was on a flight a few years ago when an attendant, who was serving us lunch, all of a sudden collapsed and landed with her face flat on the floor. She was out. Immediately the Spirit of God said to me, "Get up! Pray for her."

Some situations are a bit obvious and "in your face"; this was one of them. People started moving aside to make room for a doctor that was on that flight. He helped the lady up and put her in the seat next to me. The doctor told me, "Keep her awake. Talk to her! She is responding to you." So I prayed—both in the spirit and with my understanding. I spoke God's Word to her. Another brother on the plane came and sat in a seat across the aisle from me, and the two of us prayed this woman through. I kept my hand on her in prayer for thirty minutes as we made an emergency landing at the nearest airport. I felt prayer sustain her. During the whole ordeal, I spoke words of life to her—words of healing and the love of God. I had the opportunity to preach to everyone on the plane around me. This was one of those God moments in my life.

As I was leaving the plane, three flight attendants came to me with an offering of four bottles of wine to thank me for helping their friend. I laughed and said, "No, thank you."

Either we do something or we do not. Compassion will not let us just sit there. Later on, I received a letter from the airline thanking me for my involvement. The letter was nice, but a free ticket would have been great. Seriously, though, why do we do what we do? We are not looking for the reward that comes from man but to be involved in the releasing of God's love that changes lives.

People are hurting. They are wounded. Religion has walked right by them. Religion has said, "Well, I don't know what you did to mess up your life, but I am sure you deserved it," or, "If you had done what you should have, this never would have happened to you."

The harsh, religious-minded people cannot see the many needs all around them. Let that never be said of us. There are real victims in life. There is a real devil out there. What this world needs is people who not only believe in Jesus but who also act on His behalf—people who are willing to submit to divine "eye surgery" for their eyes to really see those around them as they never have before.

You and I must respond like the Good Samaritan in the parable. He stopped when he unexpectedly encountered a stranger in a tragic situation. Are we prepared for a divine interruption that presents us with a God-given opportunity to love and help someone in need? Are we prepared to see the world through Jesus's eyes? Are we willing to be His arms of mercy extended to those who are crying out for someone to show them a little love? Be prepared to allow the strength of His grace in you to flow out to heal the weakness in them.

Eyes of Compassion

Then Jesus went about all the cities and villages, teaching in their synagogues, preaching the gospel of the kingdom, and healing every sickness and every disease among the people. But when He saw the multitudes, He was moved with compassion for them, because they were weary and scattered, like sheep having no shepherd (Matt. 9:35–36).

Compassion gives us eyes that really see. Sight is the link between a need and the answer, between the head and the compassionate act. With mercy and grace in our hearts, we see beyond the obvious.

We see what others do not see. Compassion enables us to see people because it removes the judgmental walls around our hearts that would prevent us from acting on what we see. Love sees with an open heart and responds with an open hand. Compassion's response is always, "I will love! I will act!"

Let's be real here, though. There are some crazy people out there in life, so we must balance the stirring in our hearts with the leading of the Holy Spirit. We must follow after peace and walk in wisdom in the decisions we make. I want to stir you, but I want you to be wise and Spirit-led, not merely emotional or guilt-fueled. In no way do I intend to guilt or pressure you into performing some sort of religious duty or demand that you do this or go there. Godly compassion stirs a desire to release the love of God in a way that is led by His Spirit, not provoked by fear or manipulated circumstances.

We do not want to walk around unwilling to look at people because of what we fear God might tell us to say to them or do for them. God will not overwhelm you, and He will never ask you to do something that He won't back up. Our part is simply to obey and be available as God does the miraculous. Do not fear what may happen if you look and allow yourself to actually see people and the reality of their conditions! We have been afraid to get involved with people; therefore, we do not really look at them. We just glance and move on. Let us determine to go beyond the subtle glance and allow our eyes to be opened by the light of the Father's love for others.

People whose lives have been touched by the grace of God do not walk around cold and insensitive. Compassion responds decisively. Jesus saw the multitudes and was moved with compassion to do something about what He saw. We should do the same. I believe we should be the friendliest, kindest, most gracious people the world has ever been around. Jesus, alive in us, makes that possible.

The power of love will cause us to see what those in need cannot see but desperately need. We are able to look beyond their present moment into the future and see all the possibilities that belong to them. Compassionate eyes are prophetic eyes. Compassionate eyes do not see people as they are; compassionate eyes see others as they can be. The love in our hearts causes us to step in and say to people in need, "You may not see where you can be or the possibilities that are available to you, but I see them. Let me pray for you; let me speak a word into your life. Allow me to introduce you to a freer, healthier, stronger, future you." This is what God says about you: *"For I know the thoughts that I think toward you," says the* LORD, *"thoughts of peace and not of evil, to give you a future and a hope"* (Jer. 29:11).

When people's lives are crumbling around them, they lose hope. When people lose hope, they cannot see their future. They are so consumed with their disastrous lives that they become blinded by their circumstances and incapable of seeing a positive future. They feel alone and isolated. In order to alleviate the pain of the present moment, they look for ways to medicate it. If their pain becomes more than they can handle, many even contemplate suicide.

What people need is someone who will step into their lives and say to them, "You can have a better life. There is mercy, grace, forgiveness, healing, love, peace, and joy available for you. You can have a new start. You can have more, be more, and do more. There is a miracle for you." The great thing about Jesus is that not only does He change situations, but He also brings a brand-new nature and change of heart.

People need a shock of Jesus's love to awaken them to the glory of their future in Him. In the midst of their circumstances, they cannot see it; but we can. Like Jesus, we look at their lives and see them as they are, but we also see what they can become. Because we can see their potential future, we stop to address their present problems.

A Mad Man Meets Jesus

In Mark 5:1–20, we are introduced to a new love story in the life of Jesus. Jesus and His disciples had just crossed the Sea of Galilee and had landed on the other side in Gadara. Jesus's feet had barely touched the ground when a mad man came running toward Him. This tortured soul had been living among the dead in the darkness of the tombs. He was possessed by unclean spirits. While others feared this Gadarene demoniac and ran from him, Jesus approached him in the spirit of His Father, in the spirit of love. Jesus proceeded to cast out the devils that afflicted him and restored the man to his right mind. The man wanted to go with Jesus, but notice what the Lord said to him: *Go home to your friends, and tell them... how He [God] has had compassion on you.* (v. 5:19.)

The Bible says that when this man left that place of healing, he went to Decapolis, a region of ten cities on the eastern front of the Roman Empire in Judea and Syria. What do you think that ex-wild man was doing? He was going through those ten cities, telling everybody about the love of Jesus and how, with compassion, He had set him free from the legion of tormenting demons. When the former demoniac was delivered, he saw others as Jesus had seen him. With compassion, he was also moved to share with others that same love that lifted him up and out of his bondage. He was moved to tell them about Jesus.

When we stop not only to see what a person's situation is but also what it can be, we are compelled by the Spirit of God to open our mouths to speak hope through the Word of God. As we do this, we open the future to them. We give them something to believe in. We take them beyond past disappointments in order to resurrect their unfulfilled expectations as we introduce them to the mercies and goodness of God. Something powerful takes place when we give people the promises of God. His promises give them hope that stirs their hearts to have faith to believe in and come to the One who will fulfill the vision in their hearts for a better life. God offers, and they can receive a fresh start, healing, deliverance, and provision. The love of God, combined with faith in God, produces the miracles of God! We release that combination into the lives of others through compassion.

Compassion Heals the "Disease" of the Eyes

Do you not say, "There are still four months and then comes the harvest?" Behold, I say to you, lift up your eyes (John 4:35).

I have a passion for God's people. I want to see revival in the church, the community of believers all over our world. I want to see fire break forth from the pews and light up the world. I long to see the glory of God fill His people and empower the life of every person. I want people to know that if they need a touch from God, they can have it. I want them to know that whatever they need from God, they can receive it. I want to see miracles!

I believe that most of the time, the glory of God, the miracles of God, and the wonders of God do not happen apart from us, the Christians. When we devote ourselves to become saturated with the love, grace, and mercy of God, we will swing open the doors of our hearts. Then God will be able to release the wonders of His love to flow like a river through us into the world.

When Jesus told us to lift up our eyes, He was saying, "Look beyond where you are. Look beyond your life, beyond your situation, beyond your circumstances. Look beyond your need, beyond your pain, beyond your hurt. Look beyond your offenses. Look beyond your own limitations. Look at the fields of harvest that are *now* ready to be reaped." Others have sown, and now it is our time to reap a great harvest. Before we can become reapers, however, we must allow Jesus to restore our vision so we can have eyes to see the harvest. And that starts by walking with an awareness of the person of Jesus and the presence of His Spirit in our lives.

As I walk with an awareness of Jesus in my life, I will not allow hindrances or blinders such as offenses to stop me from seeing the opportunities all around me. It is sad how offended we can become over such little things. It is nothing but a trap of the enemy to lure us into spending our entire lives wrestling with flesh and blood. That is nothing but a waste of time to make us run out of time to reap the harvest that we have been positioned to reap. Do you realize that if we would stop wrestling with flesh and blood, offenses would have no opportunity to take root in our lives? Do you realize that the more offended we become and the more easily offended we are, the more spiritually immature and ineffective we become?

Offenses are the trap of the devil to keep us focused on the weakness in other people's lives as well as our own. If we continually focus on wrongs done to us rather than on the mercies of God and His forgiveness toward us, we will be rendered ineffective. Offenses shift our focus to ourselves and cause us to dwell on violated rights instead of our focusing on our righteousness and blessing in Him. Offenses turn our eyes toward the past instead of to the future. We have all heard certain people say the following:

"But I do not like what people have said to me."

I say, "Forgive them."

"But I did not do anything wrong. You do not understand; people hurt me."

People crucified Jesus. They betrayed Him, abandoned Him, rejected Him, falsely accused Him, ridiculed Him, spat in His face, and crushed a crown of thorns into His head. They beat His back bloody and then cruelly nailed His hands and feet to a cross.

And what was His response? He said, "Father, forgive them."

That is our example and standard. Jesus forgave not only those who were crucifying Him at that moment, but also those whose sins caused Him to be crucified in the first place—that would be you, me, and the whole world. Jesus forgave us; therefore, we can and must forgive others.

I know how difficult it can be to forgive people who have deeply wounded us. I have had opportunities for offenses. In fact, I have had to walk through many. But keeping the cross of Jesus before my eyes keeps everything in perspective. I am not taking away from or making light of the serious situations in life where we need the mercies of God to wash our hearts after being crushed through betrayals, abuses, abandonments, and attacks. I am referring to menial things that should never be exalted to a place where they can steal our joy, peace, and strength.

Jesus suffered all that we have suffered and more. Yet when somebody so much as looks at us wrongly, we become offended. If somebody does not come to our birthday party, we become offended.

How can the miraculous power of God flow through an offended heart that is hung up on trivial stuff?

"But the pastor did not greet me at church today."

Are you serious? The pastor is human; he cannot possibly greet everybody every time he sees them! Some people are just too easily offended, and it is because they are overly sensitive to the wrong things.

For the Seriously Wounded

Obviously, if you are bleeding in the middle of a disastrous situation of your own, you are not to limp around looking for someone else to heal. First, you need to regain your strength, recover, and let healing flow into you and your situation. Allow Him to restore your own damaged soul. Allow wisdom, mercy, and strength to rebuild you, taking time to become healthy and whole. It is a fact: broken people have a hard time bringing wholeness to others. You cannot give to others what you do not personally possess.

In time, as you heal and come out of your own darkness, you will find that speaking life to others, giving help and hope to others, will bring a refreshing into your own life. The words you speak to them will also refresh and encourage you. Proverbs says that he who waters will also be watered. (See Proverbs 11:25.) Then, like Peter, who said to the crippled man he and John saw at the temple gate, you can say: "I can give you what I have" (See Acts 3:6.)

Without a Vision, There Is No Hope

Where there is no revelation, the people cast off restraint (Prov. 29:18). The Amplified Bible translates this verse this way, *Where there is no vision [no redemptive revelation of God], the people perish.*

If you want a clear picture of the redemptive revelation of God, read through Ephesians chapter one. In these verses, we see that grace and peace belong to us through the Father and the Lord Jesus. Allow these verses to become established in your heart. They will lay a foundation for your future and any hope you need in life.

In Ephesians 1, we read that God has blessed us with every spiritual blessing in the heavenly places in Christ. He has chosen us in Him before the foundation of the world. We find that we have been adopted as sons with Jesus Christ. We are redeemed through His blood, and we are forgiven, accepted in the Beloved. God is making known to us the mystery of His will, which is that we have an inheritance in Christ and we are sealed with the Holy Spirit of promise as a guarantee that our inheritance will be supplied. Having this revealed to our hearts will forever change our lives. Our hope will be secure.

The clearer I see Jesus and His love for me, the more impossible it becomes for my hope to fade. I love Romans 15:13, which states, *Now may the God of hope fill you with all joy and peace in believing, that you may abound in hope by the power of the Holy Spirit.* How wonderful is it that by the power of His Spirit, we can abound in hope. If we can abound in hope, then I believe we can surely help others to do the same.

Many people today have no vision for their future. They have tried and tried to dream, have vision, and hope again. But they have been so disappointed with people and stunned by life's traumas that whatever hopes they had have faded. They tend to expect little if anything from God or anyone else. People have let them down and have not kept their word to them. Consequently, they have a hard time believing in this God who cannot lie and is *good to all, all the time.*

Honestly, when we tell some people that God is good to all and good all the time, they look at us and shake their heads, wondering, "Well, if God is so good, why is my life so full of pain?" What they have been told about the love of God does not seem to match the tribulations they are going through. The darkness of life's situations has created such a cloud over them, they can no longer see or even envision the goodness of God. They live in the tension between the goodness of God and the trouble they are experiencing. The truth is the sun of God's love has not stopped shining on them; it is just clouded by their personal pain and circumstances. Aren't you glad that hope in Him does not disappoint because the love of God has been shed abroad in our hearts by the Holy Spirit? (See Romans 5:5.) We have the joy of being both disciples and dispensers of His love and His hope.

Remember when the disciples asked Jesus, *Lord, show us the Father* (John 14:8)?

I can just imagine Jesus looking at them and scratching His head, thinking, "When will these guys ever get it?"

He responded, "How long do I have to be with you? Don't you realize that if you have seen Me, you have seen the Father?" (See John 14:9.)

Notice He did not say, "If you have *heard* Me." He said, "If you have *seen* Me. If you have *seen* the way I live, the way I talk, the way I treat people, the way I love people, the way I touch people, and the way I forgive people. If you have watched the things that I do—not just what I say, but what I do—then you have seen how the Father walks and talks and acts and treats people." In John 10:37–38, Jesus explained, *If I do not do the works of My Father, do not believe Me;*

but if I do, though you do not believe Me, believe the works, that you may know and believe that the Father is in Me, and I in Him.

Do you know what people need today? They need to see the works of Jesus. They need to see Jesus in the flesh through you and me. The Bible says, *Dear children, let us not love with words or speech but with actions and in truth* (1 John 3:18, NIV). Love is not just a just a noun; it is a verb. Love is an action. Love requires demonstration.

So many people have no vision for their future, and the Bible says that where there is no vision, no redemptive revelation of God, people perish. They give up. They quit. So many people are just "existing" today, not really living. They are alive, but they are not living an abundant life. They are not living a joyful life, because they have no hope. Jesus described the situation and responded with the answer: *The thief comes only in order to steal and kill and destroy. I came that they may have and enjoy life, and have it in abundance (to the full, till it overflows)* (John 10:10, AMP).

Having a life and enjoying it is what we want to help others expe rience. A life fully alive in Jesus is exciting and contagious! Living and spilling out the goodness of God onto others brings a joy into our own lives that cannot be contained.

When a person's hope keeps getting deferred further into the future, he or she eventually wants to give up. But when the person's eyes are opened, hope is renewed and restored. We have *seen* the Lord, so now we make Him known. Tell the world what belongs to them so they can see the glory of the Father as we have.

I realize this may seem overwhelming with so many people hurting all around us. Where do we start? In closing this chapter, let me share this familiar story.

Once Upon a Time

One time a little boy was walking down a beach. A storm with enormously high waves had passed through. Along with those monstrous waves, the high tides had caused a multitude of starfish to be washed onto the shore. As the little boy looked down the beach, he saw that there were untold numbers of starfish littering the landscape, so he started picking them up and throwing them back into the ocean.

An old man came along and asked him, "Hey, boy, what are you doing?"

"I am saving the starfish!" the boy explained excitedly. He was very happy and thrilled. There he was, the savior of the starfish. He had seen all those starfish lying there on the beach with no one to help them back into the water, and he thought, "Why let them all die? I can make a difference here. Why should I just say, 'Oh, how sad'? I have the ability to do something. I can help solve this problem."

The boy had compassion for the starfish. He saw their plight and then made a decision to do something besides just being sad.

Then the old man answered, "Are you kidding? Have you seen how many starfish there are on this beach?"

"Yes, sir."

"You're wasting your time, boy. You cannot save all those starfish."

"Well, this one I can," said the boy, holding up a starfish in his hands. "And this one I can," as he held up another. He went on with his work and simply ignored the old man's pessimism.

Some people look down the beach of life and say, "Look how many problems there are. Look how many people are wounded, sick, hurting, sad, and confused. I cannot change all that. It is overpowering. There are just too many!"

The eyes of love do not just look away. A person moved with compassion cannot just stand back and pray, "Oh, God, do something." We need to be just like that little boy on the beach who could not save all the starfish but who could save one by one until he had saved many. We need to do what we can do. We are not going to change everybody's lives. But there will be somebody whose life we can restore by introducing him or her to our loving Father. We start with the one right next to us. We may not be able to help them all, but I encourage you to reach out to help the ones you can. When each one of us is moved by compassion, together we can make a difference in this world.

When we are willing to see the world through the Father's eyes, His Spirit will equip us to reach the world with the power of His touch. We will be able to speak His words with the anointing of His voice. When that happens, the real adventures in God begin and our Christianity becomes exciting.

CHAPTER 5

THE POWER OF A TOUCH

And He laid His hands on them....

—Matthew 19:15

et's begin this chapter with a story from Matthew 20:

And, behold, two blind men sitting by the road, when they heard that Jesus was passing by, cried out, saying, "Have mercy on us, O Lord, son of David!"

Then the multitude warned them that they should be quiet; but they cried out all the more, saying, "Have mercy on us, O Lord, son of David!"

So Jesus stood still and called them, and said, "What do you want Me to do for you?"

They said to Him, "Lord, that our eyes may be opened."

So Jesus had compassion and touched their eyes. And immediately their eyes received sight, and they followed Him.

—vv. 30–34

When we read the stories of Jesus, if we're not careful to pay close attention, we will miss the little details that speak volumes. This particular story tells us about an encounter between Jesus and two blind men. In spite of the dark world that had been their home, they sensed the presence of a light as Jesus approached them—the light of the world, in fact.

In the midst of their darkness, they heard the people calling out Jesus's name. At the sound of that name, two men began to cry out in an effort to get His attention. Their cry was a plea for mercy and compassion and healing. Their desperate shout captured Jesus's attention and caused Him to stop. Jesus turned toward the two blind men and asked them what they wanted. It was not as though Jesus did not know what they wanted; He just wanted them to express their needs. At the sound of His voice, the two men asked Him in unison to open their eyes so they could see.

The biographer of this story writes that Jesus had compassion on the men; He reached out and *touched* them, and they were healed. Notice the progression of the power of the senses in this passage. Blind men cry out. Jesus *hears* them. Jesus *stops*. Jesus *speaks* to them. Jesus *touches* them. They are healed!

No one can deny the power of a human touch. Touch is a basic human need. We all crave and hunger for it. How many times have we been influenced by a hand that reached out and simply touched us? Touch communicates a great deal. Sometimes, just a touch writes a paragraph or even an entire page on someone's heart. Depending on the need, our presence and our touch, our being there for people when others have abandoned them, will communicate more than anything we could say with words.

Scientific research proves that a physical human touch can completely change the way the body functions. A welcomed touch can positively influence a person's heart rate and blood pressure. Whenever a person is touched, the pressure applied to the skin sends information to the brain; and if that touch is a love touch, it will have a healing affect.[2]

Touch can be an expression of kindness and joy. When someone is telling us a story of the horrific things he or she is going through, the natural response is to reach out and touch him or her. Holding hands is a sign of love for one another. A hug is a shared experience of solidarity, compassion, and joy. Something very powerful is transmitted from one human to another by the simple touch of a hand. When touch is backed up by the power of God, a miracle always occurs.

Electricity is to the natural world what the Holy Ghost is in the spirit world. A live wire has electricity flowing through it; a dead wire has no current flowing. We are supposed to be live wires that carry a divine current for an intended purpose. When we touch people, we have a life-giving force to transmit to them. We can bring comfort and healing through a touch. The Gospels tell us in several places that as many as touched Jesus were made whole.

The woman with the issue of blood spoke these words softly to herself: *If only I may touch His garment, I shall be made well* (Matt. 9:21). Pressing through the mass of people surrounding Jesus, she finally reached Him, and she touched the hem of His garment. The Bible says that Jesus felt in Himself that virtue had gone out of Him. We carry that same virtue, which is also described as the "anointing." It is the life, presence, power, and goodness of God in manifestation.

Compassion Manifests in Different
Ways Through Different People

Compassion is not afraid to touch people living outside of normal circumstances. If we will yield to His love that resides in our hearts, it has the ability to take us beyond the fear of getting our hands dirty. I live in the Philippines where we often experience life-altering natural disasters such as volcanoes, earthquakes, floods, and typhoons. Our church does medical outreaches when communities are faced with these challenges. I also serve as a director for Metro World Child Foundation, the largest ministry to street children in the world. These outreaches literally require me to get my hands dirty because that is what it takes to help in these types of situations.

But this is not meant to define all acts of compassion. Some people have no desire whatsoever to take a missions trip to another country or to be out on the streets with the homeless. So let's not put what it means to "touch people" in a box by giving it a narrow definition. It is like this: some people's idea of camping is roughing it in the outdoors, while others consider camping to be traveling in a thirty-foot, full-service camper and staying at a campsite powered with electricity. Everyone is different. No judgments here.

I have some pastor friends who will come to Manila but want to stay in a nice hotel and have no desire for the "missionary" experience. They are very honest about what they like and do not like. They do not have the grace upon their lives to do what I do, but they are actively involved in loving and touching people and revealing Jesus to their generation in ways that are equally powerful and transforming.

The focus of this chapter is about touching people, which after "seeing" people is the next most important step in being moved by compassion to change a life. How we go about doing that is based on the opportunities presented to us in our world. My sister, who lives in Florida, has little desire to suffer through a twenty-four-hour flight to come to the Philippines. Yet she and her wonderful husband, along with my parents, prepare a dinner for forty to sixty widows at their home every other month. Many of these ladies are in the final years of their lives. Most have almost been forgotten with little or no remaining family.

Every month, these dinners have a theme with special music and incredible amounts of food and fun. My sister and parents touch the lives of these ladies in a tender and meaningful way by esteeming them and demonstrating the love of God in a way that makes Jesus personal and real to them. It costs my extended family hundreds of dollars every month to make these special dinner events available for these widows. Although they do not actually get dirty physically, they do touch the lives of these women by stepping into the reality of their world and getting involved.

By no means do I want to put a guilt trip on anyone as I write and speak from my own life experiences. My gift and calling take me to places and people where you may never go, but the principles of demonstrating compassion that I am referring to are the same regardless of your location or the situation you may face.

My calling has required that I walk through some of the ugliest, dirtiest, most dangerous places you can imagine. I have walked in flooded streets with sewer water up to my chest to distribute food and supplies to people stuck in their homes. Dozens of people from our church were right there with me, wading through the filth and stench. After a week we had to stop our efforts because it was no longer safe to be in that contaminated water; the risk of infection was incredibly high. We can be motivated by love but we also need to walk in wisdom. I do not have to jeopardize the health and safety of my staff just to prove I love people.

On the other hand, I also realize that loving and touching people is not convenient at times. If we only look at the dirt and the danger, then some people will never receive a touch. It is not the extremity of a situation or how it may challenge us that I want us to focus on, however. I'd rather we focus on how compassion will move us to meet the needs before us.

I will never forget the time a brother and I took a long, horrible ride in a tiny Jeep to reach an isolated spot in the Philippines where some evacuees were living in a tent city. These people were there as a result of a recent volcanic eruption. It was such a long and difficult trip that for the first hours after we stepped out of that Jeep, I walked as though I were wounded because my knees had become so stiff. Despite this, once we finally arrived at that remote place, we began to lay hands on people and pray for them.

This was all a new experience for the brother who was traveling with me. He and I laid hands on one particular woman and began praying for her. My young associate had his eyes closed, but I had mine open.

I began to pray, "Father, in the name of Jesus we lay our hands on this woman, and we take authority over this leprosy..."

Leprosy (now called Hansen's disease) is a horrible, contagious disease that has been around for more than four thousand years. People who suffer from it usually have horrific skin lesions accompanied with reddish skin. In addition, they suffer from a thickening of the facial skin around the head as well as on their hands. It includes a loss of sensation in the fingers and toes.

Suddenly, my friend's eyes flew wide open in shock! Up until that time, he had not known what we were praying about for this poor woman. Suddenly, he snatched his hands away and sort of groaned at the sight of this tragic disease. But to his credit, he did put his hands back on the woman and finished the prayer.

Afterwards, both of us went to lunch. As we were walking along, we held our hands out as if they were crawling with germs. Before we ate, we washed our hands until we nearly wore the skin off of them. *Yet compassion is not afraid to touch people, even in their worst condition.*

In some of the remote villages along the rivers in the Philippines, I have watched my wife go where few would dare to tread. I have watched her crawl into homes smaller than some of our bathrooms, with seven to ten people living in a room that might be six feet by six feet. I have seen her go down into places like that and give people clothes and food. I have even seen her giving children haircuts and shampoos because everybody in the family had lice.

Compassion is not afraid of lice. Compassion continues to move and does not care whether the conditions are perfumed or if they stink. Compassion understands the power of a human touch, and it will give that touch to whomever needs it—regardless of their situation, circumstances, or surroundings.

A New Law and a New Life

For the law of the Spirit of life in Christ Jesus has made me free from the law of sin and death (Rom. 8:2). At the cross, sin was conquered;

and at the grave, death was defeated. Now there is a new law working on the inside of us; it is called the law of the spirit of life.

But if the Spirit of Him who raised Jesus from the dead dwells in you, He who raised Christ from the dead will also give life to your mortal bodies through His Spirit who dwells in you (Rom. 8:11). This new kind of life we received through Christ is a life born of the Spirit, and it now fills these mortal, earthly bodies of ours. We are born of the Spirit of *God*. If only we will grasp the full extent of that truth, our lives and the lives of those we touch will never be the same. *However, we possess this precious treasure [the divine Light of the Gospel] in [frail, human] vessels of earth, that the grandeur and exceeding greatness of the power may be shown to be from God and not from ourselves* (2 Cor. 4:7, AMP).

In the light of these verses, we understand the potential of a people walking in a divine purpose with the power of life-giving touch.

Jesus said, *I am the resurrection and the life. He who believes in Me, though he may die, he shall live. And whoever lives and believes in Me shall never die* (John 11:25–26). The real me will never die and neither will the real you if you are saved. Our bodies are getting older, slower, and more wrinkled. One day, should Jesus tarry His return, these bodies will die. But you know what? I am not a body. I am a spirit, and I have a soul. I simply *live* in a body. This body is a vessel. I want to use it to glorify God and enjoy life, but I am more than a body, and so are you.

We have a treasure inside us: the life of God indwells us. In the first letter of John, we read, *He who has the Son has life* (1 John 5:12). Second Peter 1:4 tells us that we are partakers of His divine nature. That is why, as Christians, we are a walking contradiction. We are eternal in a temporary world. My spirit is the breath of eternity clothed in humanity with my soul in the middle. I am not a human being having a spiritual experience; I am a spirit being having a temporary physical experience while I am on Earth.

What happens when I take this physical, tangible, earthly, and natural body and I touch someone? I allow the eternal part of me—the heavenly part of me, the spiritual part of me—to flow out of me into another person. My touch is a conduit for the healing presence of God. That presence is the anointing of God, the virtue of God. My touch releases a flow of that anointing to bring strength, healing, and hope into the life of somebody else.

I will not allow the devil to lie to me with these words, "Do not touch them. You might get what they have." *No! They are going to get what I've got!* I believe the scripture that says, *Greater is he that is in you, than he that is in the world* (1 John 4:4, KJV). Who is in you? The person of the Holy Spirit. He is the Comforter. When our hands are extended to release His presence to another person, our touch brings comfort. That is why our touch needs to be kind and gentle to genuinely display His heart of compassion toward those in need of His healing and peace.

Not only does the enemy not want us to engage the power of touch, he also does not want us to speak. He does not want eternal words coming out of our mouths that will release to others the virtue of divine life—the anointing of God—which has been deposited in us. In Acts 1:8, we read that we shall receive power when the Holy Ghost has come upon us, and we shall be witnesses. What does a witness do? A witness provides evidence that Jesus is alive. When we touch someone and release the power of God into his or her life, we become a witness to the *living* reality of Jesus.

Peter and John, Our Examples

In Acts 3, we read that Peter and John were headed to the Temple to pray. When they reached the gate called Beautiful, they met a crippled man begging for alms. This man captured Peter's attention, and Peter spoke these memorable words:

"Silver and gold I do not have, but what I do have I give you: In the name of Jesus Christ of Nazareth, rise up and walk." And he took him by the right hand and lifted him up, and immediately his feet and ankle bones received strength. So he, leaping up, stood and walked and entered the temple with them—walking, leaping, and praising God (Acts 3:6–9).

The news of this man's healing filtered out to all those in the city, and the church experienced a great season of growth as 5,000 people were added in one day. Everyone was happy about it except the religious leaders. They grabbed Peter and John and threw them into a holding cell. The next day, they brought these bold Christians before a religious tribunal that insisted they give an account of what they had done. These religious leaders asked Peter by what power or authority they had performed this act. Empowered with the Holy Ghost, Peter declared, *Let it be known to you all, and to all the people of Israel, that by the name of Jesus Christ of Nazareth, whom you crucified, whom God raised from the dead, by Him this man stands here before you whole* (Acts 4:10).

The name of Jesus is our authority to do the same thing in our days as He did in Peter's time. Why? Jesus is not dead. He is the same yesterday, today, and forever. He's alive, and His Spirit lives inside of us.

More Recent Opportunities

As I write this, I am still thinking about a situation that took place last year. I went to the hospital when a dear brother passed away. It was a very emotional setting as his son, a pastor in our church, had just experienced the birth of his first child in the same hospital a few days earlier. Here was a young man wanting to celebrate the entrance of a new life into the world while at the same time crying over the departure of his father. I sat next to the wife of the brother who had passed away and simply held her hand. That quiet, simple support ministered comfort and strength to her. Of course I spoke to her, but the touch told her, "I am here with you and for you. You will not be alone. You are surrounded by those who love you."

I then stood and hugged our young pastor, whom I love as a son. I offered words of comfort, but then we just stood there and hugged each other and let life and strength flow between us. All the well-intentioned words spoken that day may fade from memory, but the reassurance imparted from that quiet, compassionate embrace will never be forgotten.

As I walked to the elevator, a woman who had visited our church saw me. With tears in her eyes, she asked me if I would come see her son on the next floor. He was having some serious physical challenges. I went up to his room and there, together with his mom and girlfriend, we prayed. The Lord told me to hold him as I prayed—as a father would hold his son. As I wrapped my arms around him and prayed, I could feel the love and compassion of God flow into the young man. I could see and feel a tangible strength come into that family, as well as a sense of calm that rose up and overturned their tormenting thoughts. We all stood there, hugging and holding on to one another, letting the love of God do what it does: it invades the darkness to replace confusion, oppression, and shame with clarity, comfort, and security. When my words stopped, the power of touch continued to speak to their deepest needs.

A moment like this is when we realize that our role in a situation is to carry in and make known the One who resides within us. Do not ever think that your transforming touch is about you. It definitely is not!

In my mind, I was thinking, "Lord, whatever is needed in this young man's life, let it flow into him to refresh, restore, and renew him."

After a while, words can become repetitive and hollow, but touch can continue to give a supply of strength and support that reaches to our core needs and beyond. My greatest desire in times like these is not to draw attention to myself or to think I am what everyone needs. I simply want to make myself available to Jesus. I want to be an open channel that will give Him access to walk into situations filled with hurt, pain, and sorrow so that He can make a difference by touching through me.

We are the church, the body of Christ. We are to see people as Jesus saw them. We are to look like Jesus, touch like Jesus, and speak like Jesus. This can be accomplished because we have the ability to see and hear like He does and to feel the sentiments and passion of His heart. It is God's passion that imparts His power through our touch, just as He did through Jesus. By releasing the power of touch, we will be able to change people's lives forever.

The Power of a Touch of Jesus

The love of Jesus that He displayed for people when He walked the earth cannot be denied. That compassion, rooted deep in the heart of Jesus, always called for action, and Jesus always submitted to its call. The divine love He felt was the power to reverse the curses of human sickness and sin. Each time Jesus came across the path of those debilitated by sickness or incapacitated by sin, He reached out and *touched* them. Without exception, every touch from Jesus left the unclean cleansed, the wounded healed, the blind restored to sight, and the rejected rejoicing that God was with them.

For the Jews in the time of Jesus, the ministry of "laying on of hands," if practiced at all, had become only a ceremonial religious practice devoid of any true emotion and most certainly any power. But with Jesus, *touch* was truly an expression of divine love and human compassion. It was an empathizing, caring action backed up by the power of God, manifesting the heart of the eternal God to restore the broken and heal the wounded. Jesus's *touch* was not symbolic; it was a heart response that resonated with the richness of heaven's love and power. The touch of Jesus combined passionate affection with supernatural power.

Jesus became known far and wide for the power of His touch. People from everywhere sought Him out. Over and over again He reached out to the lepers, cripples, and prostitutes, and He *touched* them. The warmth of a human hand touching them at their point of deepest pain awakened within them a hope that had been all but lost. Combined with their faith, it allowed healing to flow. The divine touch restored their dignity and drew them out of the isolation of shame and back into the fold of humankind. Fear was dispelled, and souls were refreshed. Through Jesus's compassionate touch, doubt was dismantled, and faith was discharged to produce the miraculous when even the possibility of hope seemed pointless.

Take some time to meditate on the following verses:

Then Jesus put out His hand and touched him, saying, "I am willing; be cleansed." Immediately his leprosy was cleansed (Matt. 8:3).

So He touched her hand, and the fever left her. And she arose and served them (Matt. 8:15).

Then He touched their eyes, saying, "According to your faith let it be to you" (Matt. 9:29).

But Jesus came and touched them and said, "Arise, and do not be afraid" (Matt. 17:7).

So Jesus had compassion and touched their eyes. And immediately their eyes received sight, and they followed Him (Matt. 20:34).

Then Jesus, moved with compassion, stretched out His hand and touched him, and said to him, "I am willing; be cleansed" (Mark 1:41).

Then He came and touched the open coffin, and those who carried him stood still. And He said, "Young man, I say to you, arise" (Luke 7:14).

The anger of religious leaders did not intimidate or prevent Jesus from touching those whom religion defined as *defiled*. Lepers and prostitutes, the blind, filthy, crippled, poor, and even the dead— Jesus touched them and with compassion gathered them to Himself. There, within the arms of Jesus, the needy experienced the warmth of heaven's love and acceptance, and they received the healing and forgiveness they so desperately craved.

Jesus violated every conceivable tradition when it came to His associations with the marginalized and outcasts of Jewish society. He infuriated the Pharisees with every compassionate touch. The Qumran community of the Essenes—an apocalyptic sect in Jesus's day thought to have produced the Dead Sea Scrolls—had an unconditional law: "No madman, or lunatic, or simpleton, or fool, no blind man, or maimed, or lame, or deaf man, and no minor shall enter the community."[3]

Jesus came to shatter these manmade laws with the vengeance of heaven. Those who were rejected by the religious leaders were the very ones whom He had come to save. To the Pharisees, Jesus declared, *But go and learn what this means: "I desire compassion, and not sacrifice," for I did not come to call the righteous, but sinners* (Matt. 9:13, NAS). The Pharisees surrounded themselves with the rich, the wise, the educated, and the elite of society. Jesus, conversely, surrounded Himself with the poor, the uneducated, and the rejected. These outcasts from society became the society of the ones touched by the Master's hand.

Reach Out and Touch the World

When love rules in our hearts, we are compelled to reach out and touch others in a caring and powerful way. By the anointing of the Holy Spirit, we are responsible to initiate the touch, and God is responsible for the power that comes from our touch.

Consider these truths: What we do not love, we will not give to. What we will not give to, we will not touch. What we will not touch, we will not change.

Now I would like to tell you a story. On a certain Monday, I was on my way to the airport to depart for a ministry trip. As I was walking into the main terminal of the huge Orlando International Airport, all of a sudden a man fell down on the floor and started having a seizure. I had a plane to catch and was now faced with a potential interruption in my life. As I stated, this was on Monday, and I had just preached on boldness the day before. So here was this man, lying on the floor of that crowded terminal, gnashing his teeth and foaming at the mouth. I was in a hurry to get on with my life. I was anxious to get to the gate and relax a bit before my flight took off.

As people started gathering around the man, the Holy Spirit said to me, "*Well?*"

I thought, "But, Lord, I have a plane to catch."

"*Well!*"

His tone was clearly more emphatic the second time. What was I to do? The choice was obvious, so I knelt down to help this man. As I did, I was thinking, "I guess it will not make any difference if I make a complete fool of myself in front of all these people since I am about to fly out of here anyway."

I laid my hands on that man and started rebuking the devil. Then I began rebuking the seizure and commanding it to cease. People started staring at me, their eyes widening more by the minute. I imagined them thinking, "We do not know who is weirder, the guy having the seizure or the guy who is praying."

As I was praying in the Holy Spirit, I was thinking, "Lord, if we're going to do this thing, let's do it!" The man was writhing on the floor and groaning. I was kneeling beside him, praying and rebuking this seizure. The two of us were making some noise there. But do you know what happened? Within a couple of minutes, that seizure stopped, and the man was OK. Suddenly he sat up and thanked me for stopping to help him.

When I stood and began to walk away, you should have seen the crowd split. It was like Moses in front of the Red Sea. They were backing away from me as if to say: "Let him go, folks, before he gets started all over again!" They did not know what was going on—but the Holy Spirit and I did. That day I realized just how important it is not to avoid any situation that calls out for a human touch. One thing is certain: when God moves us with His compassion, when we will do our part, God will do His.

We have to remember that what we will not allow to touch us, we will fear or ignore. Ask the Lord to remove whatever deep-seated fear, insecurity, or prejudice that would keep you from touching others. Receive the love of God to heal your own woundedness so that you will be free to release a healing touch for others. Then watch God work.

The Attraction of a Touch

The power of a touch will attract people. Jesus became known for the power of His touch and the love that flowed through Him to *all*. This passionate devotion to the poor and needy did not go unnoticed. People streamed to Him in ever-growing numbers. Throughout His earthly ministry, Jesus continually attracted crowds of people who were mesmerized by His kindness and drawn to His irresistible grace and healing touch. This divine alliance of compassion and healing power drew the hopeful to Him day after day.

Jesus barely had any rest from the masses who desperately followed Him wherever He went. On any given day, He could be found dining in places such as the home of Simon the leper or standing in the streets protecting a prostitute from the outraged attack of religious hypocrites or having dinner with the chief tax collector, Zacchaeus. Compassion moved Jesus to walk the roadways in search of those who were lost and shunned by society. The following are just a few more examples:

> *For He healed many, so that as many as had afflictions pressed about Him to touch Him.*
>
> —Mark 3:10

> *Wherever He entered, into villages, cities, or the country, they laid the sick in the marketplaces, and begged Him that they might just touch the hem of His garment. And as many as touched Him were made well.*
>
> —Mark 6:56

> *Then He came to Bethsaida; and they brought a blind man to Him, and begged Him to touch him.*
>
> —Mark 8:22

Now It Is Our Turn

Jesus was known for the power of His touch. It is my prayer in these days that the church will also become known for the genuineness of her loving and powerful touch. I am not talking about the power demonstrated only on Sundays as we all gather together in church. I mean the power of the touch that is given by you and me out there in everyday life. We have the ability and responsibility to take people by the hand and bring them into the circle of divine love. We can allow our outstretched hands to become an extention of our Father's hands reaching out to those longing for love and mercy, so they too can be touched and transformed by the healing power of our God.

As valuable as it is to teach and instruct people in the knowlede of the Word of God, they need more than just a list of principles, instructions, and steps to follow. They need to experience the presence and attention of a God who loves them and wants to have a personal relationship with them. The ability to experience an intimate relationship with God is a completely foreign concept to most people—especially to those who have been intimidated by or burdened down with the weight of manmade, religious dos and don'ts.

Often, all that is needed to make God real to people is to provide a simple touch where you and I trust God to impart Himself into the area of their lives where they have need. As we touch people physically, God will touch them spiritually and emotionally. We are the hands of Christ to bring wholeness to the broken. Our touch can manifest His goodness to affect every area of their lives. Who would not want to have a relationship with a God who is good to all?

Many have limited themselves because they live according to their minds and their souls instead of their spirits. They are constantly living as naturally minded, and the natural mind does not receive the things of the Spirit of God. Let's stop missing out on what God is trying to speak to us and show us. We need to get out of the natural into the spirit. We no longer need to be "mere men." If we think only with the natural mind, we will cut ourselves off from the supernatural that can and needs to be extended to others.

This is where God shows up to work on behalf of ourselves and others. It is not just about our words, because what if our words are not so eloquent? Paul said in 1 Corinthians 2:1, *I…did not come [to you] with excellence of speech or of wisdom declaring to you the testimony of God.* He continued in verses 4–5, *And my speech and preaching were not with persuasive words of human wisdom, but in demonstration of the Spirit and of power, that your faith should not be in the wisdom of men but in the power of God.*

The good news we share is demonstrated through the power of God made real by a touch. I am not minimizing spoken words here, but I am accentuating the fact that touch also brings awareness of a presence greater than ours. Paul said in 1 Thessalonians 1:5, *For our gospel did not come to you in word only, but also in power, and in the Holy Spirit and in much assurance, as you know what kind of men we were among you for your sakes.*

The good news we have for others goes beyond words; it demonstrates a power to change and heal. Between the words we speak and the working of the Holy Spirit, we will usually find an opportunity to reach out and touch the hurting. This all-important touch is a connecting point, a point of contact and release. Come on! Make yourself available and watch the adventures begin.

CHAPTER 6

DO YOU HEAR
WHAT I HEAR?

[Jesus said] "If anyone has ears to hear, let him hear."

—MARK 4:23

To introduce this chapter, we will begin with a story from the Gospel of Mark:

Then one of the crowd answered and said, "Teacher, I brought You my son, who has a mute spirit. And wherever it seizes him, it throws him down; he foams at the mouth, gnashes his teeth, and becomes rigid. So I spoke to Your disciples, that they should cast it out, but they could not."

He answered him and said, "O faithless generation, how long shall I be with you? How long shall I bear with you? Bring him to Me."

> *Then they brought him to Him. And when he saw Him,*
> *immediately the spirit convulsed him, and he fell on the*
> *ground and wallowed, foaming at the mouth.*
> *So He asked his father, "How long has this been happening to*
> *him?" And he said, "From childhood. And often he has thrown*
> *him both into the fire and into the water to destroy him. But if*
> *You can do anything, have compassion on us and help us."*
> *Jesus said to him, "If you can believe, all things are possible*
> *to him who believes."*
> *Immediately the father of the child cried out and said with*
> *tears, "Lord, I believe; help my unbelief!"*
> *When Jesus saw that the people came running together, He*
> *rebuked the unclean spirit, saying to it, "Deaf and dumb spirit,*
> *I command you, come out of him and enter him no more!"*
> *Then the spirit cried out, convulsed him greatly, and came*
> *out of him. And he became as one dead, so that many said,*
> *"He is dead."*
> *But Jesus took him by the hand and lifted him up, and he*
> *arose.*
> —MARK 9:17–27

Prior to the event in the valley, Jesus had been on the mountain that we now call the Mount of Transfiguration, where His glory had been revealed to three of His disciples: Peter, James, and John. That amazing manifestation of God's glory concluded with the disciples being enveloped in a cloud, *and a voice came out of the cloud, saying, "This is My beloved Son. Hear him!"* (Mark 9:7).

I can imagine one of the disciples turning to the others with these words, "Do you hear what I hear?"

After descending from that glorious experience, Jesus and the three were confronted with a heartbroken parent, a demon-possessed child, His disciples who were frantic over their inability to do anything about the problem, and the scribes who stood nearby doing nothing but debating the situation. What a mess! Unfortunately we see this repeated over and over again when people in need come to the church looking for Jesus, expecting and needing help. Unfortunately, they often suffer disappointment when we are unable to truly meet their needs.

Rather than debating with the religious folks, Jesus compassionately spoke to the situation. People want immediate results when they cry out for help. They want someone to resolve what appears to be an impossible situation. People want help now. They want attention now. Not later, but now! Jesus entered into the situation and began an interesting dialogue with the father whose son was possessed with a demon. Jesus asked him how long his son had been in that condition, then He listened intently to the father's answer.

"Since he was a child," the father replied. Desperate, he cried out to Jesus for compassion: "If You can do anything, please help!"

Hearing the man's question, Jesus responded, "If you can believe, then everything is possible."

The father cried out, "I believe; help my unbelief." The father needed to reach beyond his most recent disappointment and tap into the faith that was within him.

That was all Jesus needed to hear. With that little mustard seed of faith, an environment was created whereby compassion connected with faith. Jesus healed the man's demon-possessed son.

The Jesus Stories and You

From this story, we learn some valuable lessons. First of all, when we are in the middle of any disappointment, everything changes when Jesus shows up. Jesus said, "Bring him to Me!" Jesus listened to the father's story about the years of torment and grief his son had suffered. Jesus made Himself available in the midst of the man's pain and confusion. We see here that when people cry out, Jesus reaches out to meet their needs.

When we combine the power of faith and the spoken word, we see what compassion will do. Jesus spoke the Word into that tragic environment of unbelief, and it created an atmosphere of faith where a miracle could take place. In this situation, Jesus showed us how even a small amount of faith, combined with the compassion of God, will produce a miracle and do the impossible.

God wants us to learn how to receive this same compassion and combine it with our own faith to enhance how we hear, believe, speak, and expect the unexpected on behalf of others. In this example, Jesus taught us not only to be receivers, but also to be givers.

The accounts of Jesus in the Gospels contain lessons to be learned, not merely stories to be memorized. For example, when the woman with an issue of blood heard about Jesus, she came behind Him in a crowd, and she said these words: *"If only I may touch His garment, I shall be made well." But Jesus…said,…"your faith has made you well"* (Matt. 9:21–22).

How did she express her faith? By making her declaration and expression from what she heard and then taking action. She touched, and she received. Have you heard of the man who was paralyzed and his friends lowered him through the roof to get him to Jesus? It says when Jesus saw their faith—the faith of his friends—Jesus spoke to the paralyzed man, and he was healed.

Then, of course, there are so many other stories: the man who sat for thirty-eight years beside the pool of Bethesda, the lepers who were cleansed and made whole, the lame who walked, the blind who received their sight, the dumb who regained the ability to speak, and the deaf whose ears were opened. When we read these stories of men, women, and children who were touched by Jesus, we discover what they heard, what they said, and how they learned to exercise their faith to receive their miracle. In their stories, we find teachings on the principles of faith and how to receive the miracle needed in our own lives; we see situations that are common to the human experience.

In these stories, we can easily see ourselves. We are the father with the troubled son. We are blind Bartimaeus crying out to see. We are the woman with the issue of blood, who spent all she had and only grew worse. We are the blind, the deaf, the bleeding, and the crippled. These stories remind us that the pain, ridicule, rejection, sickness, and oppression they felt then were no different from the bondages we face today—bondages from which we must be set free. Then, after we are healed, we can reach out to heal others.

There must come a time when we are no longer willing to remain the blind, crippled, and bound who are embroiled in desperate situations. We must come to the point where we refuse to be the ones always needing to receive. Then we can accept our responsibility and privilege to represent and reflect Jesus to the world. This does not mean we will not ever have needs; that is unrealistic. Yet even in the midst of great pain or tremendous challenge, by faith and God's grace, we can still bring answers to others. We must learn to take these same principles and be the givers, not just the receivers. As those who have been touched, we must now *give out*, not just *pull in* for our own benefit. As those who were once empty, needy, weak, broken, and wounded, it is now our turn to pour out to others from

His fullness, which we have experienced. We need to be the well, the whole, the full, and the strong in order to reach out to the empty and weak lives around us. We must rise up in faith to bring a life-altering touch to rescue and restore the blind, bleeding, and bewildered.

Just as Jesus spoke forgiveness to the woman caught in adultery, we are called to be His voice of forgiveness to those who struggle with their shame and sin. While it is important to identity with the ones who are lost, hurt, or half dead, it is more important that we learn to identify with the One who is the life giver: Jesus. As disciples of His, we should hunger to hear the voice of the Father as He heard it and to see through the Father's eyes of compassion as He saw. It matters how we see because that determines what we will allow to move us. When we see as the Father sees, compassion will move us to hear as He hears and to act as He acts. Compassion puts us into a position of faith to be givers, thus making us an answer to the needs in our world.

As I progress in my life, I do not want to always be the needy one. I want to be the giving one. Jesus has empowered me with His life and love to give. When the realization of God's abounding grace became alive in me, my faith in God motivated me to be available to others through the unlimited love of God. It is this grace that empowers me to live my life on purpose—the purpose of making a difference in people's lives. That is why I need to be a person of faith and compassion. My faith is not just for myself; it is for others.

Jesus has called us out of the multitude to be His disciples. To be a follower of Christ is to be one who does as He did and has faith to see what others do not see. *Faith is the confidence that what we hope for will actually happen; it gives us assurance about things we cannot see.* (Heb. 11:1, NLT).

The multitude showed up to be fed, to be taught, to be healed, to be forgiven, and to receive direction for life. We have all been there, but there is so much more to life than just having our own needs met. Disciples are to learn how to feed, not just to be fed, and how to heal, not just to receive healing for themselves. Disciples are followers of Jesus who learn from His example how to give forgiveness, not just how to receive it, and how to teach, not just to be taught. As we learn the other side of faith—faith that gives, not just faith that receives—we develop our ability to believe and receive from the power of God for others, not merely for ourselves alone. By giving to others what has been made real in us, we are equipped and empowered to step out of the multitude to become an avenue, a conduit of hope for people stuck in hopelessness.

Compassion Hears What Others Do Not Hear

Did you notice, in the situation with the man who brought his son to Jesus, that the Master ignored those who were in a theological debate and focused on the one in need? He listened and heard what the others did not hear. Jesus ignored the crowd but engaged the father and son who had a desperate need. Jesus had just come down from the Mount of Transfiguration after meeting with His Father. He was not seeking the situation He encountered; that situation found Him. Rather than resent the interruption that confronted Him at the base of the mountain, Jesus moved in compassion, empowered by what He had just experienced. His ears were always attentive to the Father's voice. That is why He heard the cry for help that the others had missed.

Even when the multitude left that religious wrangling to come to Him, Jesus ignored them. He was on a mercy mission specifically for that father and his demon-possessed son. We usually are drawn to the commotion of a crowd, but Jesus is drawn to the heart cry of an individual in need. Like a good shepherd, He leaves the ninety-nine sheep to seek out the one who is lost.

Do you know why Jesus heard that father and son? Because compassion listens with the heart, not the head! The head thinks, "Do I have time to deal with this situation? Do I have the ability to do anything about it? Is this important enough for me to get involved? Can I really do anything to change the situation? It might be better just to act as though I did not hear this plea for compassion and go on my way." This is the conversation between the head and the heart, the battle between convenience and compassion, between picking up our cross and denying ourselves to follow Him.

If there is ever a question about a situation, the reasoning of an unrenewed mind will always try to talk the body out of getting involved, especially if it requires sacrifice. Compassion, however, listens with the heart, not the head. Love and mercy hear what others do not hear. Jesus heard differently than the crowd or the religious people. They had other priorities, but Jesus's priorities were fixed by His Father.

I find it amazing that the majority will always tell people what they should do and usually fill them with fear and doubt for not doing it. Never listen to the multitudes. Just because the multitudes rank as the majority does not mean the majority is right. It is not surprising that the multitudes and the Pharisees were usually the focus of Jesus's rebukes. They were more concerned with self-preservation and self-promotion than they were with the needs of people or even the desires of God Himself. The noise of self-centeredness and self-righteousness always drowns out the voice of those in need.

As a community of believers, we hear what others do not hear because we hear what resonates in the heart of God. We are a people who can hear the voices of the world crying out. In fact, we have the ability to hear the sincerity of the whispered fears, "Does anybody see me? Does anybody care about me? Can anybody help change the condition of my life?" Compassion hears the sounds that others miss and then responds.

The Power of a Word

So shall My word be that goes forth out of my mouth;
It shall not return to me void,
But it shall accomplish what I please,
And it shall prosper in the thing for which I sent it.
                                                    —ISAIAH 55:11

God said that His Word will not come back to Him without producing results. It will execute what He sends it to do. The devil knows that. The seed of God's Word, when dropped into a person's heart, will always reproduce after its own kind. The last thing the enemy wants is for faith and hope to spring alive in a person's heart and then proceed out from his or her mouth. Out of the abundance of the heart, the mouth will speak. When confident expectation is mixed with those words, change will result. The devil does not want us releasing life-giving words—words of hope, words of wisdom, words of encouragement, words of faith, and words of healing. Once these words go out and are received by people, God then has something to work with in their lives so that bondages are broken, fears are brought down, and demonic spirits are confronted and cast out.

We are born again by the incorruptible seed, the Word of God, which lives and abides forever. (See 1 Peter 1:23.) His Word is absolute truth, unchanging and without error. Power is manifested when we speak words that have come from the presence of the Almighty God. That power is not based on who we are or the abilities we possess. It is released through us to connect people with the Creator of heaven and Earth, the giver of all life, the Word of God Himself!

The seed of the Word will bring forth a harvest in the hearts and minds of those who hear and receive it, producing in them the image of who Jesus is. If we are going to make an impact on the world around us, we need to know who we are and the power of the Word in us. Our words are containers that carry life, peace, hope, faith, and encouragement. We release those words by simply speaking the word that we have been given by God—not our words, but God's!

All the miracles of Jesus were a result of the commanding sound of His Word and the compassionate touch of His hands. The church is now called to be His voice and His touch in our world. What words are you speaking today? What is the result of those words? When was the last time you were moved to act on a word God gave you?

God is always moving, and He is always speaking through His Word, but we can hinder our ability to hear from Him. Receiving and releasing forgiveness is significant to our ability to receive and release words filled with the power of God. A heart that has received forgiveness and walks in forgiveness is not hardened or insensitive. We see this truth demonstrated when Jesus was invited by a Pharisee to come to his home for a meal. A certain woman, who was a sinner, entered the Pharisee's home while they ate, and she washed the feet of Jesus with her tears. Turning to the Pharisee, Jesus made a statement that holds true to this day: *Therefore I say to you, her sins, which are many, are forgiven, for she loved much. But to whom little is forgiven, the same loves little* (Luke 7:47).

When a person holds on to unforgiveness, that individual is very slow to speak words of forgiveness to others. Those who have experienced the power of forgiveness in their own lives, however, will also love much and be quick to communicate that word of forgiveness to those they encounter.

Hearing the Heart of Their Words

Compassion hears beyond the mere words people speak; it hears the heart of the words. It hears the cry of hopelessness in the words of a person tormented by fear. Compassion hears the tears concealed within a person's words. Compassion hears the heart cry of a person who aches with a longing for acceptance. The one who has ears to hear, let him hear!

When we truly hear the heart of another, it will touch our own hearts and open us up to become aware of how we can speak words that will carry the hope and healing that the person needs. Hearing the heart of another in need will motivate us to ascend above our own feelings of inadequacy and weakness so that we can tap into the power of the Word of God, which is the source of all healing and hope. We are not the savior of those we listen to; Jesus is!

It is not my job to fix everybody. In fact, I cannot fix anybody. I am not the answer to everyone's problems. But I can be an answer to someone's problem by helping them connect to the One who is. If we allow Him to flow through us as vessels of His love and power, we can release into them divine encouragement, health, strength, peace, or whatever they may need. There is no pressure on us to perform. We cannot. We are not the healers; Jesus is! He is the source; we only serve as conduits through which His Word and power can flow to others.

Hearing and Speaking by the Holy Spirit

I can of Myself do nothing. As I hear, I judge; and My judgment is righteous, because I do not seek My own will but the will of the Father who sent me.

—JOHN 5:30

For I have not spoken on My own authority; but the Father who sent Me gave Me a command, what I should say and what I should speak.

—JOHN 12:49

The Lord GOD hath given Me
The tongue of the learned,
That I should know how to speak
A word in season to him that is weary.
He awakens Me morning by morning,
He awakens My ear;
To hear as the learned.

—ISAIAH 50:4

In the first two verses above, Jesus spoke concerning the motivation behind His words and His actions. His purpose and great passion in life were simply to hear what His Father was saying, to see through His Father's eyes, then to act upon it. His authority was established in the fact that Jesus only spoke the words of His Father!

He had no other personal agenda, no hidden motives. The judgments He made were correct because they came from the highest source—God Himself.

Compassion stops us in our tracks, commands our attention, and then fills our mouths with the words of our merciful God. Those words become the source from which all our service flows to others. Every morning, we are awakened by God with the appropriate words to speak to all who cross our paths that day, because, according to 1 John 2:27, the anointing that abides within us teaches us what to say. The Holy Spirit fills us with words of hope from the Father. When we yield ourselves to Him, He gives us the specific words to speak that address the true need in the life of the person before us. That is why the apostle Paul prayed: *Now may the God of hope fill you with all joy and peace in believing, that you may abound in hope by the power of the Holy Spirit* (Rom. 15:13).

When we listen to people, we will hear that many are crying out for change. Most feel trapped inside their own lives, locked in impossible situations. They are crying out for a word that will unlock their captivity and set them free. We can see it in their eyes as they ache for a look of recognition from someone—anyone—who will see them and *care*. We can hear their cry if we listen. "Does anybody care about my situation? Does anybody see or care about the pain that I feel? Does anybody care about my marriage, my children, my physical condition, how damaged my soul is, or how lonely I feel? Does my life matter to anyone at all?"

The harassment from these fearful thoughts drives many people into such despair that their souls are like open wounds. Their emotions are scraped raw from the constant rub of rejection as they feel crushed beneath the weight of the question that torments them the most: "Does God care about me?"

"Yes!" we answer, "God cares about you! *You* are the reason God sent His Son, Jesus, to the world. In fact, *'He gave up his divine privileges; he took the humble position of a slave and was born as a human being'*" (Phil. 2:7, NLT). This is the word of hope we bring that changes everything: "God sees you. God sent Jesus to pay the price to set you free. You matter to God."

Proverbs 13:12 says, *"Hope deferred makes the heart sick, but when the desire comes, it is a tree of life."* A delayed hope breaks the heart and crushes the soul. Many people are living with sick hearts because their hope is constantly cast aside. They cry out, but it appears that no one is there to hear that desperate cry. But the words of life we speak can restore hope and fill the void in people's hearts with joy and peace that the world can neither give nor take away.

Hope is connected to the future. When people feel hopeless, they see only darkness ahead, which makes them feel even more discouraged and disheartened. But when they hear words that impart life and spark hope, that hope flickers into an optimistic thought, creating the expectation that perhaps there *is* light at the end of their tunnel. Instead of thinking about what they cannot do, they start to consider new possibilities and what they can do or become.

"I am not stuck here."

"My pain can stop."

"My confusion can stop."

"My anger can stop."

"Somewhere along the way, my life will be better."

The following is a powerful verse that gives a picture of the force of hope in a life. It speaks of the value of the hope that precedes faith:

For there is hope for a tree,
  If is cut down, that it will sprout again,
  And that its tender shoots will not cease. Though its root
may grow old in the earth,
  And its stump may die in the ground,
  Yet at the scent of water it will bud
  And will bring forth branches like a plant.

—JOB 14:7

Imagine that: at just "*the scent of water,*" life begins to spring forth from something that looked dead and hopeless. So tell me, what can our words do to produce the scent of hope in the lives of those to whom we speak? We hold the power to make a tremendous difference in their outlooks.

People's cries become an open door into their lives, giving us the opportunity to speak the words we received from the Holy Spirit. The knowledge of God's Word alive in our hearts becomes an answer for them. Faith is generated in them by hearing the Word of God, which becomes a certainty for a brighter future.

The Word Next to You

But what does it say? "The word is near you, in your mouth and in your heart" (that is, the word of faith which we preach): that if you confess with your mouth the Lord Jesus and believe in your heart that God has raised Him from the dead, you will be saved.

> *For with the heart one believes unto righteousness, and with the mouth confession is made unto salvation.*
> *For the Scripture says, "Whoever believes on Him will not be put to shame."*

For there is no distinction between Jew and Greek, for the same Lord over all is rich to all who call upon Him.
For "whoever calls on the name of the Lord shall be saved."
How then shall they call on Him in whom they have not believed? And how shall they believe in Him of whom they have not heard? And how shall they hear without a preacher? And how shall they preach unless they are sent?
—ROMANS 10:8–15

Whoever calls on the name of the Lord shall be saved. That is the promise. But with the promise, there is a potential problem. How can they call if they have not heard about the Lord who is able to save them? And how can they hear if no one is sent to them? How is that problem solved? The resolution starts in heaven where the voice of the Father, spoken by the Holy Spirit in our hearts, sends us to those in need. We answer the call, and, as we obey this commission, we receive the words to speak. It does not matter where or to whom we have been sent, God gives us a specially designed word that targets the need of that individual in a powerful way.

When we hear "the call" echoing from an angry, confused, wounded person, we stop, look, and speak that divine word. Then what happens? We give them something to believe in. By the anointing poured out through that word, we are able to move people from that place where they sit crying out for hope to a place of faith where they can believe and receive life. At that point, they have a living word to believe in and faith begins to rise in their hearts. They can now believe and accept the fact that they are loved, accepted, and valuable. They begin to understand that God is not holding their sins against them because Jesus has already paid the price. Shame is broken by the spoken word.

If people are crying out for healing, God will answer with a word, even if they are unsaved. Will God heal an unsaved person? Every person Jesus healed was unsaved. Think about that! None could be saved until after Jesus was resurrected, so of course unsaved people can receive healing. In fact, sometimes they are easier to heal, because they just trust in the mercies and the grace of God without trying to reason out everything in their minds.

Pray for your unsaved friends, and watch what God does. Healing is the dinner bell that invites them to His table. God will show His mercy, grace, kindness, and goodness. It is His goodness that brings them to repentance. (See Romans 2:4.) When they see how good He is, they will act. People do not need a religious Jesus; they need the real, compassionate, and powerful Jesus.

Listen. Sinners did not kill Jesus; religious people crucified Him. Sinners loved Jesus, and if sinners could get a glimpse of Him today, they would still love Him because He is not angry with them. We see the confirmation of this truth in one of the most quoted passages in the Bible:

> *For God so loved the world that He gave His only begotten Son, that whoever believes in Him should not perish but have everlasting life. For God did not send His Son into the world to condemn the world, but that the world through Him might be saved.*
>
> —JOHN 3:16–17

God did not send Jesus to bring condemnation to the world but to bring life, making hope and healing available for all people. The church has not been sent into the world to bring words of condemnation but encouraging words of hope and healing. Our words are spirit and life. We have something to say. Our loving God has empowered us to speak on His behalf to the world. As we speak words to them that the Father speaks to us, then touch them as His compassion moves us, God will back up the truth and reality of what we say with proof of His love for them.

CHAPTER 7

LOVE PROOFS

But God shows and clearly proves His [own] love for us by the fact that while we were still sinners, Christ (the Messiah, the Anointed One) died for us.

—Romans 5:8, amp

For nine and a half years, my wife and I lived in a certain province in the Philippines. One day we were driving down a road, and a little cement five-foot by five-foot blockhouse with bars on it caught our attention. As we were driving by the little house, I could see an arm reaching out through the bars and waving.

I thought, "Wait a minute. Stop and back up. I have to go back there."

Something about that whole scene just looked strange to me. I had seen many odd things in my life, but never anything like this. So, we backed up, exited our vehicle, and walked up to that little enclosure. As I stood in front of this little building, I was shocked.

The tiny structure had cement walls that went all the way up to the ceiling. There was a little opening across the floor that served as the toilet. The building had a window but no door. Inside was a totally naked young man who smelled like the worse sewer imaginable.

Later on, we learned from his parents that this young man was crazy, totally out of his mind. A few years earlier, he had become involved in some demonic activity and developed a habit of setting people's houses on fire at night when they were sleeping. The authorities were going to kill the young man, and because they held the parents responsible for his behavior, they were ready to kill them too.

As a result, the parents sent the young man to Manila. Doctors filled him with medications and gave him so many shock treatments that he went completely insane. Since the family did not know what to do with him, they put him inside that little cement house and closed it up so that there was no way out of it. From then on, he was imprisoned there and fed like an animal.

When I saw that, I thought, "My God, how sad." I looked at that young man, whose name was Ramon, and thought, "Lord, somebody has to do something for him." So we began visiting him, and, of course, we prayed. Believe me, we prayed. He would pick up his feces and throw it at us. It was nasty. We went there a number of times, taking authority over the devil and praying for that young man. After a while, when we visited a peace would come upon Ramon, and he would let me touch him.

His father told me that his son's hand had not been touched by anyone in years, but Ramon would let me touch him. He would sit there, right below the window, and I would reach through the bars and just touch him, and he would become calm. Then we would pray for him.

I never saw any immediate miracle or change, though we did make great progress with him. My point in this story is that compassion is proven in the things we do. We could have easily driven by and ignored this tormented soul, but love cannot ignore what it sees. Love must act; that action is the proof of the love we declare.

Miracles Start with Compassion

Keep yourselves in the love of God, looking for the mercy of our Lord Jesus Christ unto eternal life. And on some have compassion, making a distinction (Jude 1:20–21). I am not asking you to bring a demon-possessed, crazy person into your house, but I am asking you to recognize an opportunity to manifest God's love when it is presented to you. He may be asking you to show lovingkindness to a neighbor, a relative, a coworker, or someone whose problem and pain you have been ignoring week after week. I want to exhort you: if you say you have love, it is time to prove it!

Do not allow yourself to develop a dull heart, because a dull heart turns into a hard heart. I do not want that to happen—in your life, my life, or in the life of the church. God wants to bring miracles into our lives and the lives of all those with whom we come into contact. Every miracle starts with an act of compassion or prayers of compassion.

Consider the life of Jesus. When He was moved with compassion, He forgave the sinners, fed the hungry, restored the broken, and healed the afflicted. Love is not love until it is demonstrated by what we do for others. If we have a passion for something, we cannot just talk about it. We are compelled to *do* something about it. When we are passionate about something, that passion begins to consume us. It takes hold of us and motivates us to engage, reach out, and assist those who desperately need us.

Compassion Engages with the Hurting

In another part of the Philippines, there was a crazy woman who walked the streets of the city where we lived. She ate out of the garbage cans. Her body was dirty, and the clothes she wore were soiled with urine, blood, and everything else imaginable. Nobody really knew her story, but my wife, Shoddy, and I began to pray for her. We would see this lady roaming the town, and we asked about her.

Shoddy prayed, "Lord, give me that woman that I might touch her life."

One day, Shoddy was upstairs in our apartment praying for this poor woman, saying, "Lord, bring that woman into my life." Just then, the Lord told her to go downstairs. When she went downstairs and looked out the door, she saw this woman out by the garbage can, looking for lunch. So Shoddy brought her into the house. Her compassion was about to bring forth a miracle.

Shoddy took the woman to the bathroom, so she could take a shower. She then returned for a shower about every other day. Shoddy would give her just a little bit of shampoo, because if she gave her a big bottle, she would have used it all. If it had been a five-gallon jug of shampoo, it all would have been gone when this woman was through taking her shower.

The woman's body was so full of infection and disease that when we would go into the bathroom to clean up after the woman had left, there would be worms on the floor that had fallen out of her. While this woman was taking a shower, Shoddy would wash her clothes.

Shoddy also bought her clothes and kept them at our house so she could change into them after her shower. One day, when Shoddy was sleeping on the couch in the living room, she was awakened by the sound of someone pulling on and rattling the front screen door, which was locked.

Shoddy asked, "Who is it?"

A woman answered in a nice voice with good English, saying, "I am here for my shower."

Shoddy asked her what her name was, and she answered, "Jenette."

Shoddy was shocked. Despite months of coming to our house, the woman had never spoken. After Jenette took her shower that day, Shoddy sat down with her and shared Jesus; and Jenette prayed the sinners' prayer. It was the only day she ever spoke to Shoddy.

We eventually learned that Jenette had been a schoolteacher, so we sought others who could help us find out more about her life. We found her mother, who told us that one day Jenette just went crazy. All this time, we continued to minister to Jenette and pray for her. We later discovered that the drunks of the town would grab her, take her down to the river, wash her off, and then rape her all night long. After a while, she became pregnant. When Shoddy told me I immediately thought, "Oh, no. Knowing my wife, we will somehow end up having something to do with this baby."

At that same time, Shoddy was also pregnant with our first son, Ryan.

Jenette continued to roam the streets, and her pregnancy became obvious. When she went into labor, it was announced on the radio for the people involved with this lady to please come and help her. That was a shout out for Shoddy.

When Jenette gave birth to her little boy, she would not even look at him. Most likely she was in shock. It was a miracle of God that he was healthy. We brought the baby into our house, loved him, and took care of him.

Oh, the sleepless nights we had! I remember going into the room at night where we had his bed, picking him up, and saying to him, "Don't you ever stop crying? Please stop crying. I have to get some sleep, little one. Please, I am begging you. God have mercy!"

It is sad to say, but this innocent little life smelled like garbage. No amount of soap or powder could rid him of the foul odor. Just from holding him, you would begin to smell like him. It took some time for that to change.

Then, the awesome day arrived for our son, Ryan, to be born. We flew up to Manila for Ryan's birth. We left Jenette's little boy in the care of another missionary couple whom we trusted. After Ryan was born, we went back to the city where we had lived for nine years. We decided to bring Jenette's little boy back into our house to live with us.

The couple with whom we had left him wanted that little boy, and they began proceedings to adopt him. For the next three or four years, that little boy grew up next door to us and was Ryan's playmate. We were told that his birth mother had left the vicinity and had returned to walking the streets. We never saw her again, but thankfully, that little boy was adopted by the missionary couple. They knew where he had come from, but they loved him dearly. They did not care about his past, because they knew that God had a plan and a future for his life.

Today, this boy is now a grown man, the same age as our son Ryan. His birth mother came from one of the worst situations imaginable, yet this man is alive, part of a loving family, and has a great future. When he was a little boy, he was the first child in the beginning of an orphanage where eighty-five other little lives were rescued.

The bottom line with this story is that although it was inconvenient, someone stepped in to a life that was dirty and smelly to make a difference. Compassion reached out and engaged with the unlovely, and beautiful miracles were the result.

Love Activates Faith

For [if we are] in Christ Jesus, neither circumcision nor uncircumcision counts for anything, but only faith activated and energized and expressed and working through love.
—GALATIANS 5:6, AMP

In the Bible, we find examples of strong faith, weak faith, overcoming faith, outstanding faith, shipwrecked faith, amazing faith, great faith, little faith, and no faith—all kinds and levels of faith. Just as people walk in different levels of faith, so it is with love. Because of the life-changing impact that true love brings, Paul prayed for the church in Ephesians 3:17–19: *That Christ may dwell in your hearts through faith; that you, being rooted and grounded in love, may be able to comprehend with all the saints what is the width and length and depth and height—to know the love of Christ which passes knowledge; that you may be filled will all the fullness of God.*

As this level of love becomes a reality in our lives, we grow in the ability to walk in a never-ending and never-failing love. (See 1 Corinthians 13:1–8.) The agape love—or God kind of love— referred to here has little to do with emotion and much to do with self-denial for the sake of someone else. This kind of love gives without demanding or expecting anything else in return. His love flowing through us can touch the unlovable and unappealing. This love is neither natural nor human; it is the love of God shed abroad in our hearts by the Holy Spirit. When we live at this level of love, we become dispensers of God to those who need Him most.

As stated in the verse above, the Bible says that faith works by love. We can have all the faith in the world to believe for miracles, cast out devils, lay hands on the sick, or minister to people about God's miraculous provision, yet it does not matter what we may see, do, know, or bring to pass. The love of God must be the standard and motive. (See 1 Corinthians 13:1–3.)

Love motivates and gives the direction for our faith to work. Faith and love must work together because love will direct us to the right place, to see the right people with problems. The love that truly sees will position us so that compassion can move us. Love ignites our faith to come alive and bring forth both actions and answers.

If we do not have this level of love in our hearts, although we may have faith, it will not activate the power of God to the degree necessary to demonstrate His heart to the world. Do you know what happens when we do not use our faith? It becomes stagnant and weak. We talk about faith. We thank God for faith. We seek Him who is the author of our faith. But without deliberately yielding to love, our faith will not be fruitful.

Jesus said that all things are possible to him who believes. (See Mark 9:23.) When He said that, He was talking to a man whose son needed to be delivered from a demon. Obviously, faith is important. But faith alone is not all that is required to meet the needs of the people with whom we come into contact day by day. In order for faith to work, there must be passionate love that triggers the faith to produce results. *Faith is the invisible arm that reaches out and touches the invisible Jesus to bring forth visible answers to tangible problems.*

Compassion Practices What It Preaches

But [like a boxer] I buffet my body [handle it roughly, discipline it by hardships] and subdue it, for fear that after proclaiming to others the Gospel and things pertaining to it, I myself should become unfit [not stand the test, be unapproved and rejected as a counterfeit].

—1 Corinthians 9:27, amp

In this verse, Paul is saying that he had to be careful to practice what he preached. The message that he preached needed to be backed by the life he lived. As a preacher, I have to do the same. My words are qualified by my life. It is not enough to preach about love; I want to be a living demonstration of that message to all who come across my path. As I have said, our busy schedules are not an excuse to avoid the interruptions that come into our lives. Many times these interruptions are God-designed opportunities to practice the message of love that we declare. What good is the message without the manifestation of our service to others?

There are real victims in life and a real devil that afflicts them. The world does not care what happens to those who are shackled by shame and afflicted by disease. It just chews them up and spits them out. Who is going to care about people if the church does not? Who is going to reach out to them if the Christians do not? By "Christians," I mean real Christians who walk like Jesus. I do not mean just those who merely say they believe in Jesus; this world does not need that. It needs people who live how He lived, see what He saw, talk like He talked, and walk like He walked.

The world needs people whose beliefs will lead them to speak His Word and live by the same compassion that motivated Him. The world is desperately calling out for people who believe that when they extend their hands to the needy, the hands of Jesus are stretched forth through their hands. Jesus is the head of the church; we are His body. We are one; therefore, the same compassion that moved Jesus when He walked this earth is supposed to move His body today.

What will it take to make a difference in people's lives and in this world around us? It will take more than just our knowledge to fix the problems of this world. As it has been said, "People do not care about how much we know; they want to know how much we care." Having great confidence in what we do or in who we are is not what matters. It is having great confidence in the One who dwells in us. He will do through us things far above and beyond all that we can think or imagine. (See Ephesians 3:20.) In fact, He will amaze us with what He wants to do through us!

The Lord is looking to shock and amaze us with His goodness. He is looking to astound us with the wonders His love will perform. In order for Him to do that for us, He needs our obedience. He needs us to have willing hearts to yield to the love of God and to practice what we preach.

Our Lives Speak Louder Than Words

We have this treasure in earthen vessels, that the excellence of the power may be of God and not of us. We are hard-pressed on every side, yet not crushed; we are perplexed, but not in despair; persecuted, but not forsaken; struck down, but not destroyed.
—2 CORINTHIANS 4:7–9

People may argue with what we say, but there can be no arguing with what we show. When our lives repeatedly demonstrate the peace of God, even when we face problems, people will want what we have. When they see us walk in joy despite the difficulties of life or walk in love even toward those who do not love us, the world will take notice and know there is something different about us.

They will seek us out to rescue them from their painful circumstances. They will seek us, not because of who we are, but because of who we carry! If we will step forward, trusting in God to step with us, He will be the One who changes and rearranges their situations. He will be the One who gives them renewed hope until they long for and receive the life of God, which will fill their hearts with the kind of treasure that fills yours.

Love Destroys the Works of the Enemy

For God so loved the world that He gave His only begotten Son, that whoever believes in Him should not perish but have everlasting life.

—JOHN 3:16

For this purpose the Son of God was manifested, that He might destroy the works of the devil.

—1 JOHN 3:8

If we put these two verses together, we come to this conclusion: God so loved the world that He gave His Son to destroy the works of the devil in the lives of people. By conquering sin and death, He brings grace, freedom, and life to all.

In John 10:10, Jesus said that the thief comes to steal, kill, and destroy. But whatever work the enemy may use to try to steal, kill, or destroy in your life, Jesus has come to destroy that specific assignment of the enemy against you, so you can live an abundant life. If the enemy is seeking to steal from you through lust, Jesus came to destroy the power of lust because it will ruin your life. If you are bound by fear, Jesus came to destroy fear's grip, because fear will cause you to miss the blessings of God. Whatever the work of the enemy may be, whether it is anger, jealousy, envy, or pride, Jesus came to destroy it, because He knows that if it is left alone, it will eventually consume us.

Jesus came to break the power of Satan in your life so that you do not have to be a servant or a slave to sin. That's the good news. Jesus came to give you freedom so that you do not have to be manipulated like a puppet by the schemes or strategies of the devil. Jesus came and cut those strings that would keep you attached to the world, and He set you free.

He also came to save you from the deadly influences instigated by Satan's control. Pain, poverty, sickness, disease, fear, oppression, and confusion are subject to the authority Jesus gave us through His name. Regardless of what this world may offer, Jesus came to offer us something better, something so much more wonderful. In John 16:33 He said, *These things I have spoken to you, that in Me you may have peace. In the world you will have tribulation; but be of good cheer, I have overcome the world.*

In the writings of the apostle John, we read: *He who is in you is greater than he who is in the world* (1 John 4:4). He goes on to say, *For whatever is born of God overcomes the world. And this is the victory that has overcome the world—our faith. Who is he who overcomes the world, be he who believes that Jesus is the Son of God?* (vv. 4–5).

God sent His Son, Jesus, to overcome the world and to destroy the works of Satan, the god of this world. Those of us who believe in Jesus are sent by Him to carry out the work He started. As He taught us to overcome, our mission is to bring that overcoming life to others. We are now the ambassadors of Christ, and as His representatives, we are committed to live from a place of victory because of what Jesus has done for us. Then we are to go and reflect that overcoming triumph to our world.

Compassion Shows Mercy

Blessed are the merciful, for they shall obtain ≠mercy.
—MATTHEW 5:7

The Greek word for *merciful* in this verse is derived from the Greek word *eleeō*, which means, "to have mercy on; to help one afflicted or seeking aid;...to bring help to the wretched; to experience mercy."[4] As you read your Bible, I encourage you to mark the word *mercy* every time you see it. Seventy percent of the time, the word *mercy* used in the New Testament is derived from the same Greek word that is translated *compassion,* which is from the Greek word *splagchnizomai.* This is a most interesting word because it means, "to have the *bowels* yearn, that is, (figuratively) *feel sympathy,* to *pity:* have (be moved with) compassion."[5] The Greeks believed that the bowels or spleen area were the innermost part of a person, so this would be a moving of the innermost part of a person toward another.

When people called out to Jesus crying, "Lord, have mercy on us," they were saying, "Lord, have compassion on us. Lord, let our situation, condition, and position in life touch You in such a way that You cannot ignore us. Let it cause You to stop, stand still, and do something about it. Lord, spare me from the pain and suffering; spare me from harm and trouble."

That is what mercy does; it spares people from pain and suffering and delivers them from harm and trouble. That is why the blood of Jesus was sprinkled upon the mercy seat before the Father, where it continually cries out on behalf of all mankind, saying, "Mercy!" The blood speaks, calling God not to hold our sins against us and to come to our rescue. This blood asks God to see, stop, and consider our situation and bring change to the pain in our world because it has been poured out on our behalf.

Heaven's Applause

And whatever you do in word or deed, do all in the name of the Lord Jesus, giving thanks to God the Father through Him. And whatever you do, do it heartily, as to the Lord and not to men.

—COLOSSIANS 3:17, 23

As this verse states, whatever we do in word or deed, we are to do it in Jesus's name as unto the Lord and not for the applause of men. The proof of our love is demonstrated in the mercy and kindness that we show to others, but we do not seek men's favor; we seek to honor God. It is all for His glory.

In Matthew 10:42, Jesus said that anyone who gives someone even as much as a cup of cold water will by no means lose his reward. Then in Luke 6:23, He said that our reward is in heaven. Jesus also told us that when we pray in the secret place, our Father rewards us openly. There are many verses that speak of blessings and rewards. Isaiah 1:19, for example, reads, *If you are willing and obedient, you shall eat the good of the land.*

I enjoy blessings as much as anyone does. Let's be real here: we all like being blessed and rewarded for our efforts and diligence. Blessings and rewards come from both heaven and Earth, from God and from man. We are seen and appreciated by some and ignored or taken advantage of by others. Choosing to live a life pleasing unto God is born out of desire and not the result of man's imposed requirements.

Everything that comes to us, even that which has been deposited into us, we need to steward well. Blessings we receive on Earth are to be used in this natural and temporary realm, but we sanctify them and increase their fruitfulness when we choose to invest them in touching and influencing people for eternity. The Bible says that it was Cornelius's giving and praying that came up as a memorial before God. (See Acts 10:31.) Heaven's rewards extend beyond the temporal realm of time; heaven's rewards are eternal and are the true treasures we need to lay up for ourselves.

I do not know about you, but I want a reward that is eternal. People can bless me down here, and it is greatly appreciated; but I do not focus on man as the source of my reward. I want a reward from my Father in heaven. Hebrews 11:6 tells me that *He is a rewarder of those who diligently seek Him.* One reward for seeking Him is a greater awareness of His presence in my life.

The first time the word *reward* was used in the Bible, God told Abraham that He was his exceedingly great reward. (See Genesis

15:1.) Abraham's reward was not a *what* but a *who*—God in his life. Wow! What a reward! Then, in the New Testament, *reward* is first mentioned in Matthew 5:46, then again in Matthew 6:1. In these verses, Jesus informed us that our rewards come not only from how we love people, but also from the motive of our hearts.

The compassion that flows from our lives to others is not to be expressed with the ulterior motives of gaining the awards and praises of men. We are givers, not takers. What we do is not motivated to achieve the applause of people; our desire it to receive the reward of knowing we have lived in a way that gave God pleasure.

When we are moved by heaven's love, we will be consumed with a passion to help others. Some of them will love us for the rest of their lives. Others we help will love us for a while; but over time, they will either forget or perhaps turn away from us. Some will even criticize us. But none of that matters. We walk in compassionate love to honor God, not to be praised by men. Hebrews 6:10 states: *For God is not unjust to forget your work and labor of love which you have shown toward His name, in that you have ministered to the saints, and do minister.*

You May Be Criticized, but That's OK

In closing this chapter, let us take a look at an event in the life of Jesus. It is one of the more famous stories in the Gospels. Some of us even sang a song about this story when we were children in Sunday school. It is the story of Zacchaeus.

In Luke 19, the author tells us that Zacchaeus was a hated tax collector and very short in stature. When Jesus came to his village, Zacchaeus had to climb a tree and hang out on a branch in order to get a glimpse of Jesus as He was passing by. As soon as Jesus was under that tree, He stopped, stood still, and looked up at Zacchaeus. Staring him in the eyes, Jesus said, *Zacchaeus, make haste and come down, for today I must stay at your house* (Luke 19:5). Immediately Zacchaeus climbed down and led Jesus to his home where he prepared a dinner for Him, the disciples, and some of Zacchaeus's friends, who were also tax collectors.

Now, let me explain something. The tax collectors were despised and considered heathens by the pious people of their day. They were hated because of their collaboration with the Romans to exact as much money as they could from the Jewish citizens. So when Jesus had dinner with such people as tax collectors and prostitutes, He was severely criticized by the religious leaders. However, that made no difference to Jesus. His eyes were focused on those who needed His touch.

Jesus was always going to dinner with the wrong crowd, but what was He doing at those get-togethers? He was there to reveal God's mercy to ones who did not deserve it. That is what mercy is all about: God's love being shown to those who are not worthy.

Jesus's mission was to minister, heal, love, and forgive the rejected and the ostracized in Jewish society. He was always doing good deeds on behalf of His Father. In Acts 10:38, we read that God anointed Jesus with the Holy Spirit and with power. Jesus then went about doing things that were good. Everywhere He went, He manifested the goodness of God. He healed. He loved. He forgave. He delivered. Everything He did was good, yet some people still talked negatively about Him.

No matter how much good we do for others, there will always be those folks who want to talk about us and criticize us. But we cannot allow the world to steal our compassion from us. Our heart can be perfect and right before God, and people will still look at it, judge it, and be critical of it.

The motive behind our acts of compassion is born out of hearts that passionately love God and fervently love people. Do not let anything or anybody keep you from fulfilling this divine calling.

CHAPTER 8

TWO CROWDS AT THE GATE

"I have set before you life and death."

—Deuteronomy 30:19

We discussed the following story earlier, but there is another important angle that I would like to point out to you at this time.

Now it happened, the day after, that He [Jesus] went into a city called Nain; and many of His disciples went with Him, and a large crowd. And when He came near the gate of the city, behold, a dead man was being carried out, the only son of his mother; and she was a widow. And a large crowd from the city was with her.

When the Lord saw her, He had compassion on her and said to her, "Do not weep." Then He came and touched the open coffin, and those who carried him stood still. And He said, "Young man, I say to you, arise."

So he who was dead sat up and began to speak. And He presented him to his mother.

—Luke 7:11–15

As Jesus traveled to the little village of Nain, a town in Galilee, a huge crowd was following him. *Nain*, which means, "pleasant or green pastures," was about a day's journey southwest of Capernaum, where just the day before Jesus had healed the centurion's servant.

When Jesus and the crowd entered the city gate, they were confronted by a funeral procession in progress. A widow's son had just died. According to Jewish tradition, a quick burial was required to avoid ceremonial uncleanness by inadvertently touching the dead body. Like most Jewish funerals in those days, the family and friends of the family would tear their clothes, accompanied by intense demonstrations of loud and extreme mourning.

Now, I would like you to imagine that you are there with the two huge crowds. One crowd, possibly as large as five to eight thousand people, is following Jesus and His disciples. They are rejoicing over the love and power Jesus demonstrated in the miracle healing at Capernaum. The other large crowd is probably about the same size since most of the city is participating in this funeral. These two crowds approach in opposite directions and are about to converge, but each crowd is expressing a different mood.

The first crowd—the one with Jesus—is following life, joy, peace, healing, hope, and renewed expectations. This crowd is celebrating. They have experienced His miracle-working power. Whether they have been healed, fed, or delivered from the devil, they have cause for great joy. Life is in this crowd. They are not mourning. They are not sad. They are not weeping because they are around life, hope, and mercy. They are around Someone who brings provision, healing, and the presence of God.

Now observe the atmosphere in the other crowd; it is totally the opposite—a tragic sight. A young widow is weeping over the death of her only child, and most of the city is crying and mourning with her. There is no peace; instead, there is confusion, worry, and fear concerning the future. Somewhere in the middle of this crowd is the widow weeping over the death of her only son, wondering what will become of her life now that he is gone. Any parent would be moved with compassion by observing the widow's pain. First, she has lost her husband, and now, her only child. What is she going to do? Who will take care of her? The crowd of grieving mourners offers no answers for her future; they just walk with her. The rhythmic beat of wailing and weeping only increases the solemn mood enveloping the entire group.

Now visualize Jesus and His crowd moving toward the gate of the city. At the same time, the funeral procession is coming toward Him from the other direction. The forces of life and death within these two crowds are about to collide as both groups reach the gate of the city. *Jesus is about to ruin this funeral!*

Finally, the two crowds approach. I can imagine how, as they stop to inspect each other, Jesus emerges from the crowd that is full of life. Luke wrote these words about that moment: *When the Lord saw her, He had compassion on her* (Luke 7:13). Thousands of people are gathered around, but Jesus sees only *one* person: the grieving widow. His eyes are focused on this woman embroiled in great pain. Looking beyond the crowd that is surrounding her, the Lord directs His attention exclusively to her. The Bible does not say that Jesus saw a *crowd*. It says that Jesus saw *her*.

Compassion moves Jesus to reach out and touch the open coffin carrying the dead son. This horrifies the Jewish leaders who are present that day. To touch a dead body, or the coffin carrying that person, is a violation of their law. Yet despite this "violation," Jesus says, *Young man, I say to you, arise* (v. 14). To the complete amazement of the grieving crowd, the young man instantly comes to life, sits up, and speaks!

Luke said that a great fear came upon the people, followed by a time of worship for the glorious healing that had taken place. The miracle they have just witnessed is undeniable. The mood of the crowd immediately changes as life has conquered death. The people begin to glorify God, declaring that Jesus is a prophet and that God has just visited them. Miracles will change the mood of any crowd, moving them from grief and doubt to worship and faith.

A Picture of Believers

There are thirty-seven recorded miracles of Jesus in the Gospels, which is but a glimpse of all He said and did. John 21:25 says, *And there are also many other things Jesus did, which if they were written one by one, I suppose that even the world could not contain the books that would be written.* As we look at the accounts in the Gospels, we see not only how Jesus lived, but also how He desires those who believe in Him to function in our world today. These accounts reveal what the love and the goodness of God can do in a world where people are hurt, wounded, bound, ashamed, and even dead. These accounts are about real people with real problems, yet each received real love and real answers from Jesus.

Funerals happen every day around the world, but the event we have just imagined with this particular widow stands alone in its uniqueness. When Jesus saw the woman, He looked intently at her. He saw her pain and was moved with compassion. This is an awesome story of the difference between the two crowds. Yet, it is more. *To me, it is actually a picture of the church and the world.* In one crowd there was life. Coming from the opposite direction was a crowd that carried death. There is only one thing that distinguishes believers from the world, and that is the presence of God, His life within us. *He who has the Son has life* (1 John 5:12). The church is a community of believers that is to be a place where life is found and where doubt, despair, and the fear of death are dispelled.

I love this crowd. I love the church—the community of believers who carry life. As we carry life with us, we will always confront death, sadness, and sorrow. Our journey in this world will always encounter the unavoidable contradictions of life and death, joy and sorrow, faith and doubt. What matters most is how we walk that journey. When we are faced with the contradictions, which will we embrace? Life or death?

Life hurts—have you noticed? Life is full of pain. Even if you are walking in the crowd of life, you will be confronted by people who are going through challenges. Pain, hurt, disappointment, worry, and fear are common and inevitable experiences in life. As we encounter them in our day, it is no different than when Jesus met the funeral crowd that day. The people were coming toward Him from the opposite direction, carrying a different atmosphere. That crowd needed an encounter with life. We can be that encounter for people as we reach out to them with His life and transforming power that reside in us.

We do not gather as the church, a community of believers, because we are the pretty, perfumed, and polished who have it all together. We come together because we have met Jesus. We come to worship Him and to hear His Word. We come to fellowship with and encourage each other and to give thanks for the answers that come into our lives.

Perhaps, however, when you come into the gathering of God's people, you might be feeling sad, hurt, or wounded. You might wonder what people who believe in Jesus are so happy about. Or you might be at home thinking, "Well, I do not want to go to church. My attitude is bad." No problem! Bring your bad attitude to church. That is no reason to stay away. Come as you are. Bring your stinky, sorry, sad disposition to church because His Presence there is greater than whatever is on you. Instead of wallowing in your situation, come to church where you can receive a change in perspective, answers to your questions, and the support of other Christians.

Believers come together because we have had an encounter with the goodness and the grace of God, not because we are perfect and do not have any issues. We simply trust that He who has begun a good work in us will complete it. (See Philippians 1:6.) Each one of us is a work in progress. Even as we move forward with this crowd that is carrying life, we ourselves will be confronted by circumstances that will challenge this faith we carry.

Shoddy's Story

A few years ago, my wife, Shoddy, was diagnosed with tuberculosis and large B cell non-Hodgkin's lymphoma at stage two. This was just three months after she had recovered from dengue fever and pneumonia. As soon as Shoddy was diagnosed, we did everything we knew to do. We trusted God, we prayed, we sought good doctors, and we totally changed our eating habits. I joined Shoddy in eating whatever she ate. I lost twenty pounds, and I was not even sick!

Actually, many of us would do well to change what we eat. I am serious! If you have high-blood pressure and you are eating ten burgers a day and a few pounds of bacon per week, it is time for a change! If your blood sugar is out of control and you drink twenty Cokes a day, you need wisdom to make better decisions nutritionally so you will not have to use your faith to offset the health consequences of your reckless food choices.

When Shoddy was given that diagnosis, we began to research and find everything we could about how to battle the cancer. I told everybody, "Do not go to Shoddy with all the remedies and books you have to help." People were flooding us with books, CDs, DVDs, and all of their advice. As a husband trying to protect Shoddy, I told our people, "Do not go directly to her; she is overwhelmed. Everything is to come through me. I am the filter." We were taken back by the immediate response of our people and their concern, support, and desire to help, but suddenly, I was bombarded with more cures, remedies, websites, and causes for cancer than I could read in a couple of years.

One night I attended a five-hour seminar solely on the topic of food. I learned about the healing properties of eating fruits and vegetables as part of our daily diet and the value of juicing. As we continued to pray and trust God for Shoddy's healing, we did everything we knew to do in the natural. That included making the choice to eat healthily, but we also made the decision for her to undergo chemotherapy.

I told Shoddy countless times every day, "You are in a constant state of recovery unto complete wholeness." I would lay hands on her at night and speak over her, "You are in a constant state of recovery unto complete wholeness." She would fall asleep with those words in her ears. I would speak those words over her even as she slept. Most of the time, Shoddy would go to bed early because she was so tired and weak from the treatments. She wanted me next to her so that at any time she could reach over and feel that I was there beside her. A touch brings security and peace along with the assurance that one is not alone. When she would stir or awaken, she would hear those words being spoken over her, requiring every cell to recover continually unto complete wholeness.

During this time, Shoddy had to stare death in the face. She was not afraid of death, but she constantly had to choose life. You know, everybody wants to go to heaven, but nobody wants to die. There was a period of time when our worship team came into the house. They love Shoddy, and they would come to encourage her and to minister to the Lord, creating an atmosphere for the presence of the Lord to rest upon her in a tangible way. Shoddy would be lying on the couch very weak, and the keyboard player would come in along with the guitar player. Together, they just worshiped.

During that time, I gave them clear instructions: "Sing songs of victory, faith, and hope but nothing about the glory. Do not sing anything about heaven, because if she gets a glimpse of heaven, she will leave me to go there."

Then I prayed, "Jesus, I want You to touch her. I want You to speak to her, but please do not show Yourself to her, because if it is between You and me, she will be gone."

Every single day, the most important thing in our house was to have the presence of God there. The presence of God is still the most important thing in our house. We learned that if we build a solid foundation when it is peaceful and calm in our lives, we will not be shaken and crumble when calamity and crisis come.

Storms will come; and most of the time, we will have no warning as to when they will hit. Therefore, in a time of calm, it is imperative that we build our lives in such a way that when crisis hits, we will have enough stability and strength to withstand the storm. This matters to all of us; because *we will rise to the level of our preparation, and we will stand according to the strength of our foundation.* A difficult situation of testing is not what causes us to rise up; it just gives us an opportunity to respond to what God has already made available to us. It is our trust in Him and in what we believe that gives us the ability to rise up, stand up, and speak out. *Trials do not make us; trials reveal us.* Trials do not perfect us. The Word of God and the Spirit of God perfect us as we go through trials.

As Shoddy was going through her recovery from cancer, tenderhearted people would say to me, "Pastor, I believe that Jesus is going to heal Shoddy because she has given thirty-four years of her life to serve Him and she loves this nation." Or they would say, "We know that God is going heal Shoddy because He has a great future for her."

When Shoddy heard this, her reply was always the same. It was not about what she had done. It was about her keeping the focus on Jesus, the cross, His blood, and what He had done for us all. *Healing belonged to Shoddy because of what Jesus had done, not because of anything she had done.* We also reminded these well-meaning individuals that He was not going to heal her because she had a great future still ahead of her. Everyone has a great future in Him! Healing already belonged to her because of who Jesus is and the fact that He already bore her sicknesses for her. (See 1 Peter 2:24.) The focus had to be on Jesus *alone.*

While Shoddy was undergoing treatment, a test revealed that she possibly had an incurable tumor behind her heart. The doctors were talking about the need for open-heart surgery. At that time, they told us that the tumor had become the most serious issue, and the cancer was suddenly secondary. In our church, we conduct a Saturday night service, along with four services on Sunday. After we received the report about the tumor, at the end of the last service on a Sunday, we went into a time of prayer and worship for two and a half hours just for Shoddy.

As we were finishing prayer that Sunday, the Spirit of God said to me, "*Do this again next month, but this time, pray for the other people in your church because not everybody gets the attention that the pastor's wife receives. Everyone else in here is just as valuable and just as important as Shoddy. The same price was paid for them that was paid for her, but they do not have the benefit of focused corporate prayer like she received in this prayer meeting. So next month, I want you to conduct the same kind of prayer meeting for anybody and everybody who needs a miracle from Me.*" So we did, and tremendous miracles occurred!

Later, when Shoddy and I returned to the doctor regarding the tumor, they performed several tests but could no longer find it. Nothing was there! A week later, she continued with treatments for the cancer.

You might say, "Maybe there was nothing there to begin with."

Well, whether it was not there or God took it away, I really do not care. Whether it was a blood clot that dissolved, a tumor that disappeared, or a misdiagnosis entirely, it does not matter. All I know is my wife is now strong, healthy, and whole, and we will finish our days together.

That was not an easy period in our lives. We had much to confront during those dark days, especially in the beginning. We rejoiced through it all and continued to rejoice when the complete wholeness came to her life. We learned to live with the attitude of that crowd with Jesus, the ones who chose to celebrate life.

No one volunteers for difficult times like we walked through, but when times like that come to challenge us, we can choose which of the two crowds we will follow. There will always be some in the crowd who have had loved ones depart to be with the Lord, but because of Jesus, it is still a win-win situation. *To live is Christ, and to die is gain* (Phil. 1:21). God's Spirit comforts us with the knowledge that to be absent from the body is to be present with the Lord, which is far better, the apostle Paul said. (See verse 23.)

Often as we are traveling, Shoddy will share her testimony of healing. Afterwards, people will come up and ask her, "How did you win that battle? How did you deal with it?"

Her response is always the same: "The first thing we tell everyone is this: When you get sick, do not hide it. If you get sick, you have not done anything wrong."

Many people have been fed wrong information. There are those out there who teach that if a person becomes sick, he or she may have opened the door to the devil or perhaps sinned. People hear that and become ashamed because they think it is their fault or that their faith is not strong enough. Or they are afraid that if they share what they are dealing with, people will bombard them with negative comments. Shoddy always tells people not to worry about that. Instead, it is important to find those you trust and with whom you can be honest and share with them what you are going through.

When a person is sick, it is a very personal matter. Surround yourself with people of faith who will encourage you, pray with you, and walk with you through the journey. They are the crowd that will connect you with the same life and power that greeted the widow and raised her son from the dead. Their joy, peace, and confident expectation will be the atmosphere you want around you when difficult times hit. They will not only carry life to you, they will also lift and carry you.

A Third Crowd

Now as they went out of Jericho, a great multitude followed Him. And behold, two blind men sitting by the road, when they heard that Jesus was passing by, cried out, saying, "Have mercy on us, O Lord, Son of David!" Then the multitude warned them that they should be quiet.
—MATTHEW 20:29–31

The Greek word translated *mercy* in verse 30 also means "compassion." So these two blind men were actually crying out to Jesus, "Lord, have compassion on us!" Do you know what compassion is? It is active mercy—mercy that produces change. As we have mentioned previously, nothing about compassion is passive.

In the light of our examination of the two crowds mentioned earlier, in this scenario we see a third crowd, one that was trying to get the two blind men to just shut up. (See verse 31.) When you are crying out for the mercy of God, ignore those who tell you to be quiet. In fact, get louder! I do not mean just with your voice; let your heart cry out for the mercies of God. They are available to you. Here is my advice: *Don't ever listen to the multitude. You cannot follow it.* Today the multitude will cry out, *Hosanna to the Son of David! Blessed is He who comes in the name of the* LORD! (Matt. 21:9); and tomorrow the multitude will shout, *Crucify Him!* (Mark 15:13). Multitudes can be very fickle.

The multitude goes along with the majority, believing that the majority is right. Do not do that! You can die by following the majority. Just out of curiosity, do you know who Palti, Igal, or Sethur were? No, I didn't think so. They were just a few—the majority—of the ten spies who gave an evil report to Israel and caused an entire nation to die in the wilderness. On the other hand, I'm sure you do remember Joshua and Caleb. They were the minority who boldly declared, *We are well able* (Num. 13:30). Joshua and Caleb had a different spirit. It is the spirit of the crowd you are in that counts, not the size of it.

A Vivid Example

One time, my wife and I were trying to cross a busy street in a certain city in the Philippines, which, by the way, takes an enormous amount of faith! We were standing on the street corner with a crowd waiting for the traffic light to change so we could cross. All of a sudden, the crowd started moving across the street. So naturally, we went along with them. Bad move!

Suddenly we found ourselves in the middle of the street with cars coming at us from this way and that way. There were cars everywhere bearing down on us. We looked up at the traffic light, and it had not turned green; it was still red. We had not even bothered to look at the light before we crossed. Everybody else was moving, so we just moved along with them and got ourselves into trouble. Do you know what happens when you blindly follow those in front of you? You get run over just like they do!

We did not take the time to look out for ourselves in that situation, and it nearly cost us our lives. Too often we do not take the time to check things out for ourselves; we fail to listen to what our own hearts are saying about a particular situation. We must be careful of the multitude, lest we get run over by a bus.

Everybody is in one crowd or another. We are either following life, or we are following death. The crowd we are in will determine how we spend our time, energy, talent, and money. It will establish what we become involved in and the purposes that will be carried out in our lives. I love the life crowd, and I have chosen to identify with them and walk with them. Keep in mind: it is also important that we never allow our choice to join the life crowd to isolate us or cause us to be afraid to step out of that crowd in order to touch someone who is not in it.

Jesus Instills Expectation

Here is something we need to see: when Jesus saw the crowd following death, He did not step aside and say, "Wow, that is really sad." There are times when we are going through tough times and we are barely making it. Even with all of our faith and all of our believing and all of our praying, we feel as though we are doing everything we can just to keep our heads above water.

Then we cross the path of somebody who is under pressure just like we are. In that moment, we are tempted to avoid the person's eyes. We do not want to get involved with someone else when we are going through our own problems. We think, "I cannot really give them attention because they might expect something from me." We may feel so inadequate or beaten down ourselves that we do not want to get involved, because people might want or need us to do something that we have not been able to do for ourselves.

Have you ever pulled up to a stop sign and seen someone begging for food? It is common in Asian countries and is becoming more and more common in the United States as well. I am sure you have seen the signs in your own town: "I am homeless." "Need food." "Need money." "I can't feed the kids. Help!" "Can't pay the bills!" Some are so bold that they will come up to a car, knock on the window, and look inside trying to make eye contact with the driver.

How many of you know that when you pull up to that kind of situation, you do not stare at the guy? If the guy looks at you, you do not look back; because if you just look at him but do nothing, it would be considered rude. If he makes eye contact with you and you continue to look at him, you are giving him something: *the opportunity to expect something from you!* So rather than continue to look at that person, you may tend to look away. Have you recently looked away from someone in need? When we disconnect our sight, we usually disconnect our hearts. I am not saying you have to engage every beggar that approaches you. What I am saying is that instead of having an automatic response of rejection, we are to be open to what the Spirit of God would have us to do. Thankfully, Jesus never disconnected His heart.

When Jesus saw the grieving widow who was about to bury her only son, He looked at her and had compassion. We will never have compassion on a person we are unwilling to look at. Anytime Jesus had compassion, He always brought change into the situation. He raised the level of expectation for all those who came into contact with Him, because He was willing to look them in the eye and acknowledge that He saw them and recognized their need.

When we allow something to touch our hearts in the way it would touch the heart of Jesus, we might become nervous. And nervous is good, because nervous usually means we have encountered a situation that is above and beyond our ability to fix. It makes us nervous when we realize that if God does not do something, nothing can be done. We are just going to have to trust Him. Nervous can also mean it is beyond our comfort zone, but that is a good place to be; God always wants to get us out of our comfort zones.

Compassion will allow what we see to move us in such a way that we just cannot leave that situation in the same condition in which we found it. We are compelled to bring change to that situation. *That* is compassion!

Compassion was God's response when He saw us. He could not leave us in the same tragic condition in which He found us. He had to bring change. In Hebrews 4:16, we read these words that reassure us of God's love for us and of the value of prayer: *Let us therefore come boldly unto the throne of grace, that we may obtain mercy and find grace to help in time of need.* As we come to the throne of grace, we receive compassion. When we approach God, He sees us as we are and is prepared to open to us the treasures of His compassionate love.

What God sees in us so touches His heart that He *cannot* leave us in the same condition in which He finds us. He *must* bring change into our present situations. This compassion—this refusal to leave people in their tragic condition—is what we are called to bring to our world. If we—the community of believers—look away, the world has no hope! When our compassion becomes greater than our fears, we will be quick to bring people to the One who can heal the ache in their hearts and the sickness in their bodies.

Speak the Word to Change the Situation

When we see others through Jesus's eyes, we will be touched by their situations and then we will speak, just as He spoke to the young widow. He saw her and had compassion on her. He spoke to her and to the situation. If we do not open our hearts to be touched, we will never open our mouths to speak; because it is out of the abundance of our hearts that our mouths speak. It starts with our first being willing to look.

Other things we have to deal with before we can speak are the fear-based thoughts that challenge us, trying to convince us not to say or do anything. For example, fear of embarrassment may cause us to think: "I do not have what it takes to meet that need." Let me tell you, it is not *what* you have that matters—it is *who* you know. The Greater One inside you is more than enough to meet their needs. Fear of disappointment will also try to keep us quiet and inactive. Listen, if we pray for someone and it does not work, that person is not going to be worse off. We should never be afraid of taking a chance to reach out to others and to speak God's Word to them.

An Opportunity I Had

I remember one time when we were in a small town to conduct an evangelistic healing meeting. We went to a little hardware store to buy some materials, and there I saw the cutest little girl. She was the daughter of the owner, who was Chinese. Her eyes were so horribly crossed that it made me dizzy to look at her. I felt impressed to ask her father if I could pray for her. I told him who we were and why we were in town. I knew he was a Buddhist; I could see the typical statues displayed in the store.

The thought came to me, "What if it doesn't work?" Then I thought, "Well, she will not get any worse. What do I have to lose, and why am I thinking about myself when she is the one who has the need?" We prayed for her, and Jesus instantly healed her eyes. Her crying father picked her up and came to our meeting that night.

Now, Back to Our Story About the Widow

The Bible says that Jesus *saw* her. He had compassion on her, and He said to her, *Do not weep* (Luke 7:13). What an incredible statement. Jesus told her not to weep when she had every right to cry. Her husband was dead. Now, her only son had died. She was sad, hurt, lonely, and distraught. She was probably dealing with all kinds of fear, but Jesus spoke the Word to bring change into her situation.

You and I, as believers, will have opportunities to make an impact on people's lives. That impact will not come by our just bringing people to church with the hope that one of the pastors can help them. No, some of the greatest miracles that will touch and transform lives will not happen inside of a church building; those miracles will take place outside those walls in people's everyday lives.

As I have already mentioned, the majority of Jesus's miracles seemed to be interruptions as He went through His days. I believe there are divinely orchestrated interruptions waiting for you and me—God ordained appointments we will have opportunity to step into. If we will just see these opportunities through His eyes, allow them to touch our hearts, and allow the knowledge of God's Word we have inside of us to speak, then we will also see miracles take place in people's lives through us.

As carriers of life, we will always be confronted with hurting people—people who are dealing with pain and loss, people who feel as though they have no options or solutions. But as a community of believers, walking in the crowd that is following Jesus Christ, we have answers. We have life. We are not intimidated by difficult situations or dark circumstances.

I do not know about you, but I am no longer willing to allow fear to cause me to look away and draw back from the needy people around me. I have purposed in my heart: I am not going to let my past define my future actions. I am in the crowd following Jesus for a reason. Since I am in the crowd that is following Him, I am following life, peace, mercy, and grace. To follow Jesus is to follow help, hope, healing, and provision. As the people who follow Jesus and carry life, whenever we contact the crowd that carries death, we can and must present them with life. We have the hope and healing they need. We cannot simply step aside to let them pass while we shake our heads and say, "How sad."

We do not need more knowledge to make a difference. We have already received more than most of the world has ever heard. We need to move on from just hearing in order to obtain more knowledge; we must step into believing and taking action!

Do you know why many Christians become bored and lose their excitement for the things of God? It is because all they do is listen and listen and listen and listen some more. They have books, CDs, and DVDs by the roomful. They watch Christian television, they look on the Internet, they follow Twitter and blogs in order to read more, but many rarely do anything with what they have heard. They have accumulated a great deal of knowledge, but they take little time to apply it! Many are too busy attending seminars and bouncing around from one church to another in their search for more. They are hearers of the Word but not doers of the Word. A doer of the Word will move from hearing to applying what he or she hears, from reading a text to taking action. The only way to activate in our lives what we have learned is by *doing something* with that information!

What will strike a new spark in your Christian life, moving you from apathy to active involvement? You will exit the door of disinterest when you begin to walk in what you know, acting on the truths you have already learned. When that change begins to take place in your life, a freshness will spring up, and then flow out from you into the lives of others.

A Word for the Dead

"Do not weep." This appears to be a strange, almost inappropriate instruction for a widow who had just lost her only son. Why should she stop sobbing? She had lost everyone dear to her, and her hope for the future had died with them. But the next thing Jesus did was to take away her tears. He turned from the woman toward her son, touched the coffin, and commanded the young man to arise. To the great amazement of all those watching, the young man was raised from the dead before their eyes!

Notice that first Jesus spoke to the living, and then He spoke to the dead. He spoke a word to prepare the widow to receive a miracle. Then Jesus demonstrated that the power of His Word had no limits as He delivered the young man from the grip of death. Permit me to offer you this assurance: if there is anything in your life that you think is dead, do not despair. Jesus can resurrect it. Dead goals, dead dreams, dead desires, lost hopes, lost opportunities, and all those regrets that you feel are suffocating you—Jesus is able to raise them to new life by the power of His Word.

You might say, "Well, Pastor, I need a miracle in my life. I need so many things, but I just do not deserve them." I have a revelation for you: You are right. You do not, but then again, nothing you have ever received from God is based on what you deserve—beginning with your salvation. We do not deserve Jesus, but we have Him. *For **by grace** have you been saved through faith* (Eph. 2:8, emphasis added). The mercies of God are new and fresh every single day. Great is His faithfulness. If I am unfaithful, He remains faithful because He cannot deny Himself or His Word. Grace and mercy are opposites in a way. I have heard it said this way: The definition of *mercy* is "*not* getting what you deserve." On the other hand, *grace* is "*getting* what you do *not* deserve."

Our Bible is not a story or history about great individuals. It is a story about a great God who used ordinary men and women to do great things. That is the crowd we are walking in—the crowd of ordinary people doing great things because we follow a great God who has done great things within us, for us, and through us. We are not people who have never felt pain, sorrow, or disappointment, but we follow the One who stepped into the midst of our pain with healing. He brought joy to our sorrow and restored our hopeful expectation where disappointment had been the norm.

God can restore what is lost and revive what is dead—every time! He is the resurrection! He is the life! You may have made decisions that you think have taken you too far off course, but you are not too far gone. God can bring you back! In Joel 2, the prophet declared, *So I will restore to you the years that the swarming locust has eaten* (v. 25). So what if you are far away from where you should be? Perhaps you have made some unwise decisions, wasted years, or done some foolish things. Your relationships, marriage, or family may look beyond repair, but let me tell you this right now: God loves you, and He sees your situation! No matter what you are facing or how you may feel, God has a word that can bring life back into your circumstances.

Touch Your City

Not every broken life you encounter will be as obviously desperate as a woman with her dead son in a funeral procession. You may come face-to-face with just one person in a crowd. Yet when you see that person's need, I encourage you to have compassion on that individual and allow God's power to flow to him or her. When this happens, a part of your city will be affected. Your city is waiting to be touched and changed by the hand of compassion, and most likely that change will take place one person at a time.

I am confident that God wants to touch the tragic conditions of our cities and He wants to use our hands to do that. Someone may say, "Well, Pastor, that's your job." Yes, it is my job, but it is your job too. It is the responsibility of every believer, and that includes all of us. The Great Commission is not for a few; it is for *all*. Tomorrow, when you go to work, to school, or to the grocery store, you will meet someone who is crying out for a compassionate touch. It might be in the produce section of the grocery store between the apples and the bananas where you see a person with slumped shoulders, a lowered head, and a sad countenance. You might simply ask, "Are you OK?" The person will either brush you off or open the door for conversation. There is little to lose and so much to gain. Of course we never want to invade a person's space or overwhelm an individual.

Give him or her a chance to invite you in. If the person does, kind words and a loving touch can do miracles.

These are the moments when life becomes exciting, when we have the opportunity to change the mood of those caught in the grip of death and despair. I am not telling you to interrupt the next funeral you encounter, but there are many "walking wounded" around you whose lives could be healed and transformed if someone would just stop and share the love of God with them through a word or a touch.

Life becomes exhilarating when we abandon the safety zone and ask God for adventures. The most depressed people I know are predominantly self-focused. In their minds everything is, or should be, about them. They are the center of their own lives. My friend, you are not to be the center of your life; Jesus is. He came to make you the center of His life.

Recall our Bible story of the two crowds that met Jesus at the gate of the city. By the end of the narrative, only one crowd followed Him. If you will not hesitate to step out in faith, allowing God to do the extraordinary through you, those who are in need of His grace, Word, and power will want to follow you as they followed Jesus.

CHAPTER 9

GENEROSITY

As a result of your ministry, they will give glory to God.
For your generosity to them and to all believers will prove
that you are obedient to the Good News of Christ.

—2 Corinthians 9:13, nlt

What does it mean to be generous? Is generosity tied only to the financial realm of life, or does it apply to every area? As we return to the story of the Good Samaritan, I want to look at the three attitudes reflected by the passersby in this parable: the thieves, the priest, the Levite, and the Samaritan. I also want to examine how they responded to the man in need. Each one of us will either display or encounter these attitudes in our life's journey. We should ask ourselves this important question: "Of these people, whom do I most resemble?"

We will start with the thieves. They represent those who have the attitude, "What's yours is mine," those who are willing to use lies, manipulation, guilt, exaggeration, or whatever is necessary to turn a situation to benefit themselves at the expense of others. They grab what they can, when they can, draining the energy or resources of those around them with little or no conviction or concern for others. They use people and value themselves first. Such individuals look for opportunities to take rather than to give. When we come into contact with a person who has a thief mentality, he or she will leave us weakened and diminished, having less than we had before.

All of us have been wounded at one time or another in our lives by thieves. These robbers have stolen not only tangible goods such as businesses, money, or valuables, but they also have robbed us of our dignity, esteem, families, and relationships. Many people today are desperately trying to find and rebuild healthy, positive self-images that were stolen by those who devastated them with the thief's attitude. Some people will rob a person with their hands, whereas others will steal from people by using words. The danger of the thief is that he is not only willing to take from existing generations, but he also will also rob any legacy that would be passed down to the generations to come.

The second type of attitude in this parable was displayed by both the priest and the Levite. Their attitude was, "What's mine is mine." This mentality says, "I have the ability to make a difference in someone else's life, but I choose not to. My time, talent, and treasure are for my benefit alone, not yours." Selfishness and self-preservation dominate this way of thinking, overwhelming any notion of meeting the needs of others. People who embrace this mentality are not willing to inconvenience themselves for anyone else. They focus on guarding what they have due to the fear that they will not be able to replace what they give away. They do not derive joy from blessing others, and they do not comprehend the value of sowing seed. They deny others in order to guard what they have gained so that they can retain it exclusively for themselves.

Unfortunately for the man who lay bleeding on the roadside, the attitude of "what's mine is mine" governed the behavior of the priest and the Levite, who happened to be the first two people on the scene. Although these two did not take anything from the victim as the thieves had, they did nothing to help him either. They ignored his obvious need and kept walking, unwilling to allow their hearts to be moved to action.

It is true that there are times—especially for us husbands and fathers—to be responsible and guard, maintain, preserve, and protect our families. Yet when a protective mentality crosses the line to self-centeredness or selfishness, it is wrong.

As we encounter situations in life where we see a person in need, like the wounded man on the journey, we must ask ourselves, "What can I do to make a positive change in the situation?" There is a time when we must deny ourselves, pick up our crosses, and follow Him. Sometimes it will cost us to bless and bring increase to another's life. I do not know about you, but if it is within my power to make a difference, I do not want to leave people the way I find them, and I certainly do not want to leave them with less than they had before I came into contact with them.

If we are self-absorbed in our thinking, it limits the blessings of God from being poured out through us onto existing generations. We might think that our unwillingness to respond does not take anything away from anyone, but it does not add anything either. As for the notion that nothing is taken away, consider this: our unwillingness to become involved very well might remove the last shred of hope from the person who is desperately needing care or concern. What we do—or do not do—matters.

Finally, in this story we are introduced to the compassionate heart of the Samaritan. His attitude was, "What's mine is yours." This selfless way of thinking represents the lives of those who are generous. The Samaritan's actions reached beyond his own needs or pleasure. He lived with and for a purpose. That same purpose should reside in us. We are to live a life of serving, giving, and distributing. We need to step back and look at what we have in our hands and ask ourselves, "Can what I have make a difference in someone's life?" When we choose to release what we have on behalf of others, we open our lives to receive joy. Jesus said, *It is more blessed to give than to receive* (Acts 20:35). There is a true and unique delight that results from watching our giving enlarge the lives of others.

God is looking for such vessels. He is unwilling to do without cheerful givers who will selflessly give their time, talent, and treasures to uplift, encourage, strengthen, and enlarge the lives of other people. (See 2 Corinthians 9:7, AMP.) Our attitude should mirror that of the Good Samaritan who took pleasure in bringing assistance to one in need. When we encounter people who care, who are enthusiastic givers, who add to our lives and enlarge us, they encourage us, leaving us bigger, stronger, and more emotionally stable. They revive our dignity and self-esteem. They restore wholeness to wounded lives through their generous spirits. It should be our goal to allow giving to permeate every area of our lives until we produce a legacy for generations to come. This is the attitude that will change individual lives and transform this world.

When Jesus finished sharing the story of the Good Samaritan, He left us with a command that should become our heart's motivation: *"Go and do likewise"* (Luke 10:37). Are you ready?

The Generosity of Jesus

As we examine the life of Jesus, we see that the spirit of generosity permeated everything He did with His time. Whether feeding the multitudes, forgiving those full of shame, or healing the broken, Jesus gave extravagantly, especially in the way that He gave Himself for us all. He was given to us—without reservation—by the Father. From the time of His baptism (when He came out of the water at the river Jordan), to the day He came out of the tomb, He never stopped giving.

When we gain a revelation of heaven and eternity, it positions our hearts in such a way that we are willing to give not only what we have, but also who we are. Do you believe in the purpose of God to the point that you are willing to give the most expensive asset you possess? Are you willing to give yourself and your time to benefit others?

Time is a very precious commodity, especially when it comes to time spent with children. I have learned that money means little to them. What registers in their love account is time on Daddy's lap, a story before bed, playing together outside, or just spending time—or should I say investing time—together. That is what children remember and what produces a lasting reward.

The same is true of people in general. You will find that the only thing some people really need is for us to give them a little attention to communicate that they are valuable. When we are willing to stop for just a moment to listen and give of ourselves, people feel as though they matter because we have given them something precious. Time is like money; it can be hoarded, or it can be spent or invested. Most of us only will invest in things that we consider worth the risk. The truth is this: regardless of people's status in life, they are valuable. Every person we meet is an eternal spirit. We have the opportunity to influence and affect them in a lasting way by what and how we choose to invest in them.

Generosity causes us to give of ourselves as Jesus did. His love for you moved Him to lay down His very life for you. This should prompt us to ask ourselves, "How generous am I in my willingness to give of my time and money?" This world will never be touched by those who are unwilling to give of themselves in extravagant ways. The world is changed when we are motivated by our love for God and people. God intended love to be the distinguishing mark upon all of His disciples. It is love that will make us stand out to the world and identify that we are His. Jesus said it this way in John 13:35: *By this all will know that you are My disciples, if you have love for one another.*

The love of God is selfless and overwhelmingly generous. Generosity should be the defining quality of everyone who calls themselves a Christian. It motivates us to focus on what we can do to bless people, rather than focusing on what it will cost us. You have probably heard the saying, "You can give without loving, but you cannot love without giving." John 3:16, the most famous verse in the Bible says, *For God so loved...that He gave....* The ultimate expression of God's love was revealed by His willingness to give. The foundation for God's giving is His love. The groundwork for our giving is also our love and compassion. Obligation, manipulation, and persuasion are not appropriate reasons for us to give; our giving should flow out of a love for God, His purpose, and the people He has created.

One erroneous teaching that is influencing people today is the belief that one's level of giving will determine what he or she receives in return. Now, I do believe that as we sow we will reap. My concern is that some are so preoccupied by their return that they seem to lose track of what their giving is accomplishing in the lives of others and how it is advancing God's kingdom in the earth. Our giving is so much more than a numbers game whereby we measure the percentage of our return. It is so much more than a heavenly stock market where I give and then check out what my quick return will be. My true joy is in my giving, not in the measurement of what I receive. I truly believe that we cannot out-give God, but we should never give based on what we believe will become our measure of return. Consider this: God gave us His Son with no guarantee whatsoever of what our response would be or what we would do with His gift. Unfortunately, there are many who have rejected or not received this gift of amazing grace, but it never stopped or deterred the Father's generosity in giving us Jesus. God gave because He loved. Period.

I do not believe God wants His people to be stingy. When we have something in our hands to give, we should be willing to share with those in need around us. When we become more focused on what we can receive rather than what we have to share, there is a problem. However, when love is fluid in our lives, it helps break the barriers of selfishness and stinginess. When faith is added to that love, it helps break the obstacle of fear. Loving and giving are inseparable; they are at the very core of God's nature and character.

As His character becomes our character, joy will come alive in our hearts concerning the area of giving.

True joy does not come from seeing the residual effect that giving multiplies back to us. The real joy comes when we witness lives change as a result of our generous acts. Although I have already shared this verse written by the apostle Paul, I believe it bears repeating: *I have shown you in every way, by laboring like this, that you must support the weak. And remember the words of the Lord Jesus, that He said, "It is more blessed to give than to receive"* (Acts 20:35). God help us all to receive a revelation of that truth in our hearts.

Generosity Sees Beyond the External to the Eternal

Over the years, I have watched how loving generosity will cause congregations and individuals to sacrifice and give to nations and people they may never see personally. This kind of generosity has resulted in cities, countries, and a generation of people being touched and changed for eternity.

Compassion and generosity have motivated churches and individuals to sow into Shoddy and me for over thirty-four years. They have loved not only what we do, but also who we are, embracing us and our family. I will be forever grateful to those who looked beyond the preaching, the schools, the outreach, the building of a church, and all the ministry activity to see a man, a husband, a father, a woman, a wife, a mother, and three children. They saw our family.

This loving generosity has also been manifested when people have graciously responded during times of disaster to help our church reach those dealing with the atrocities of floods, typhoons, earthquakes, and volcanoes. These are people and churches who continue to believe they can make a difference in this world through their giving. These are the churches that continue to grow and prosper even in the midst of their own financial challenges and have become avenues, streams, and distribution centers to the world. Because of their generosity, they will not lack. Proverbs 22:9 says, *He who is generous will be blessed, for he gives some of his food to the poor* (NAS).

The world of the generous gets bigger and bigger, while the world of the stingy gets smaller and smaller. I do not know about you, but I want to see my world increase. I believe my giving brings increase to other people's worlds, and God brings increase to mine. I love Proverbs 19:17, which says, *He who has pity on the poor lends to the* LORD, *and **He** will pay back what he has given* (emphasis added). It is the best investment strategy the world has ever known. Whatever we give to those in need, the Lord says *He* will repay. He assumes it as His own personal debt, which He will repay in full.

One powerful Scripture passage that reveals how God feels about our generosity is Matthew 25:31–40. In these verses, Jesus talked about who will enter heaven:

> *When the Son of Man comes in His glory, and all the holy angels with Him, then He will sit on the throne of His glory. All the nations will be gathered before Him, and He will separate them one from another, as a shepherd divides his sheep from the goats. And He will set the sheep on His right hand, but the goats on the left. Then the King will say to those on His right hand, "Come, you blessed of my Father, inherit the kingdom prepared for you from the foundation of the world: for I was hungry and you gave Me food; I was thirsty and you gave Me drink; I was a stranger and you took Me in; I was naked and you clothed Me; I was sick and you visited Me; I was in prison and you came to Me."*

> *Then the righteous will answer Him, saying, "Lord, when did we see You hungry and feed You, or thirsty and give You drink? When did we see You a stranger and take You in, or naked and clothe You? Or when did we see You sick, or in prison, and come to You?" And the King will answer and say to them, "Assuredly, I say to you, inasmuch as you did it to one of the least of these My brethren, you did it to Me."*

What a powerful view of Christ's heart for the poor: "Whatever you do unto them, you do unto Me." How many of us would like to think that if we were to see Jesus in need, we would serve Him, that our response would be to give Him our best, most valuable gift we had to offer? We have that chance each time we choose generosity as our response to people; we are choosing to serve the Lord.

Love Makes You a Giver

> *When He had called the people to Himself, with His disciples also, He said to them, "Whoever desires to come after Me, let him deny himself, and take up his cross, and follow Me. For whoever desires to save his life will lose it, but whoever loses his life for My sake and the gospel's will save it."*
> —MARK 8:34–35

These verses mention the desire to follow Jesus before they address the price of following Him. Before we talk about the word *deny*, let's talk about desire. He is my desire. Following Him, knowing Him, and loving Him is where it all starts for me. When my focus is on Him, I will make right decisions.

What possible reason would cause us to deny ourselves to benefit others? Only one: love. Love is the only force that will motivate us to sacrifice and lay our lives on the line for someone else. A true disciple knows this and yields to it. Jesus put it this way: *Greater love has no one than this, than to lay down one's life for his friends* (John 15:13). Believers today should be the most generous people on Earth because we understand that the true purpose in living is not about gaining, but giving.

Generosity Requires Good Stewardship

When compassion prompts us into action on behalf of others, it moves us beyond speaking or touching into the realm of giving tangible resources. The principle of stewardship helps us understand that what we have has been delegated to us—not given to meet our needs and wants alone, but to use to serve the needs of others. As stewards, we are to be responsible and faithful with our gifts, abilities, talents, and blessings that have brought increase to our lives.

For some, that increase manifests in notoriety because of a position or status attained. There is nothing wrong with enjoying blessings that come our way or with being grateful for certain recognitions we receive. As stewards, however, we realize that blessings and notoriety provide us with a platform from which we can serve in a greater capacity. Blessings come into our lives not merely for our enjoyment and pleasure; our lives hold a deeper meaning and purpose. God entrusts us in many ways, and how faithful we prove to be in the small areas will determine the degree to which God will increase us to steward even more.

Personally, I desire to be a channel through which God can meet the needs of others. The Dead Sea provides us with an example of the opposite mentality. It has much flowing into it, but nothing flows out from it. It is full of minerals, but those riches have to be mined. Its supply remains contained within itself instead of flowing out and increasing and enriching other waters. I suppose that is why it is called the *Dead* Sea. *Life*, as it was intended, is defined by giving and receiving, not just taking in and never giving out.

Good stewards have to maintain a consistent flow of giving out; there is a purpose for everything that comes to them. God is looking for faithful stewards to whom He can entrust much. He is looking for those who want to be a distribution center to their world. When you have proven to God that what He gives you can flow *through* you, He will have no problem getting anything *to* you.

Stewardship is also taking what you have—even when it seems insignificant compared to the need at hand—and merely making it available. When the disciples questioned how they could possibly meet the needs of the tired and hungry multitude, a little boy simply made his lunch available. Jesus did the rest.

Our perspective plays a great role in our stewardship. If we look at situations from an earthly-minded perspective, we will maintain a limited viewpoint, placing too much importance on that which is merely temporary rather than what is eternal. Heaven's perspective, on the other hand, provokes us to be faithful stewards so that God can get involved. He ensures that what has been entrusted to us in the natural will do more than just meet an immediate physical need.

Good stewardship applies natural resources toward eternal purposes that establish the kingdom of God. Using natural commodities such as food, money, or material goods to meet needs and make God real to others is the way we can use the natural to produce spiritual fruit. Earthly works can make heaven real to others, and temporary things can be used to establish eternity in the hearts and lives of others. We all have been entrusted with something; how we steward that something will determine its value. Why? Because use is what produces increase.

True Prosperity

The true definition of prosperity means to flourish and to be successful in *everything* you do; it is not limited to the financial realm. Traditionally, we relate prosperity to financial wealth that is acquired through success in business. Economic success produces abundant wealth for the prosperous person to live happily without fear of lack or need. The financial wealth of a prosperous person is usually the result of commitment, hard work, taking risks, utilizing brilliant strategy, or a really nice inheritance.

Money accumulated in these ways provides us with the ability to be generous. But true prosperity is simply a means to an end. For years the body of Christ has enjoyed teaching that God wants to prosper His people. I believe this is right and true; however, it is not the end of the story. There is a *purpose* for that prosperity, and that is for us to be generous. Prosperity defines what is coming in, while generosity identifies what is going out. *Our world needs more than a prosperous church; it needs a generous church!*

If the flow of our prosperity is directed toward meeting our needs only, then we run the risk of damaging our souls. How do I know this? Because concerning Israel, David wrote, *And He gave them their request, but sent leanness into their soul* (Ps. 106:15). One cannot count the number of seminars, meetings, CDs, articles, and books that have been produced on prosperity. I do not believe God is against our prosperity, but again, financial wealth is simply a means to an end. God forbid that our pursuit of financial abundance is motivated solely by our desire for personal gain and not for the purpose of what we can also accomplish for the kingdom in our world today.

My friend Judah Smith, senior pastor of The City Church in Kirkland, Washington, holds a Generosity Conference every year. The one I attended was the first conference I had seen that emphasized *generosity*. I love this concept, because the focus is on "such as I have, I give." It is all about what we are expecting to give out, not just what we are expecting to see come in. If we make no apologies for prospering, there certainly can be no hesitation in our generosity.

If I am faithful with what I have and generous with the tangible resources that I possess, will He not entrust me with the true riches of heaven? The natural encompasses how we behave and act in the world we live in. How do we handle our money? How do we handle the natural, physical, and temporal blessings in our lives? How do we treat people where we work? How do we act toward our spouses and children? How faithful are we at our jobs?

If we are faithful with these things in our natural, everyday living, then God can trust us with things in the spiritual realm, such as gifts, anointings, authority, spiritual insight, revelation, and favor. I believe God uses our lives in the natural world to prove our faithfulness so that He then can entrust us with spiritual riches. If He cannot trust us with the natural, the earthly, and the temporary, how can He trust us with the spiritual, heavenly, and eternal? I pray that in all our prosperity, we are not found lacking. If at each level of prosperity we only increase our level of living, rather than increase our level of giving, we open the door to leanness in our souls. Let us not fall victim to this condition but rather be mindful of this: while the world hears us speak of prosperity, it cries out to see our generosity!

The Grace of Giving

In 2 Corinthians 8, Paul talks about the grace of God upon the Macedonian churches. This is a great example of generosity empowered by grace:

> *Moreover, brethren, we make known to you the grace of God bestowed on the churches of Macedonia: that in a great trial of affliction the abundance of their joy and their deep poverty abounded in the riches of their liberality. For I bear witness that according to their ability, yes, and beyond their ability, they were freely willing, imploring us with much urgency that we would receive the gift and the fellowship of the ministering to the saints. And not only as we had hoped, but they first gave themselves to the Lord, and then to us by the will of God.*
> —2 CORINTHIANS 8:1–5

The churches of Macedonia were planted by Paul on his second missionary journey, where he established churches in Philippi, Berea, and Thessalonica. In order to reach these cities, Paul traveled along the Mediterranean coast through Syria and across Turkey until he arrived in the northern part of Greece. He preached the gospel in these three cities and had great success among the Gentiles and the Jews. During his time there, he told the churches about the great economic crisis among the believers in Judea due to a famine that plagued their area. With an open heart and generosity, the Macedonian churches contributed to that relief fund, even though they were in great distress themselves.

Paul used the example of these churches in Macedonia as a way of motivating the church at Corinth to allow this work of grace to be manifested in their midst as well. Through Titus, Paul exhorted the Corinthians with these words: *But as you abound in everything— in faith, in speech, in knowledge, in all diligence, and in your love for us—see that you abound in this grace also* (2 Cor. 8:7).

This grace of giving and generosity needs to be as obvious as our faith, speech, knowledge, and actions motivated by love. Our giving is a true demonstration of our love. It is compassion in action and the powerful combination of the grace of God mixed with the love of God. Demonstrating our love is the purpose for our prosperity. Beyond the getting and the gaining, it is the sowing into and the growing of the kingdom in people's lives.

The first time Paul was with the Corinthian church, the people made a commitment to help their Christian community in Jerusalem; however, they had not yet fulfilled their promise. Paul concluded his message by exhorting the church to complete what they had desired to do the year before: to help the struggling saints in Judea. He endeavored to move them from a place of readiness to complete that effort. God's grace working in our lives empowers us to perform.

Our *intentions* will never result in people being saved, healed, or fed. It is the love of God in *action* that brings these things to pass. For the intentions of the heart to be meaningful, they must result in taking the steps necessary to follow through on those intentions.

Generosity Affects Your Future

But this I say: He who sows sparingly will also reap sparingly, and he who sows bountifully will also reap bountifully. So let

each one give as he purposes in his heart, not grudgingly or of necessity; for God loves a cheerful giver. And God is able to make all grace abound toward you, that you, always having all sufficiency in all things, may have an abundance for every good work. As it is written:
"He has dispersed abroad,
He has given to the poor;
His righteousness endures forever."
Now may He who supplies seed to the sower, and bread for food, supply and multiply the seed you have sown and increase the fruits of your righteousness, while you are enriched in everything for all liberality, which causes thanksgiving through us to God.

—2 Corinthians 9:6–11

Verse 6 in the Amplified Bible reads this way, *[Remember] this: he who sows sparingly and grudgingly will also reap sparingly and grudgingly, and he who sows generously [that blessings may come to someone] will also reap generously and with blessings.* Paul makes it clear what should be the motive in our giving. It is so that *blessings may come to **someone*** (emphasis added), not to ourselves. The by-product of that giving is that we are blessed, but that should not be the primary motive. Because we want *others* to be blessed, we give. This motivation to be generous is counter to everything we see in our culture. Only love thinks that way—God's love.

I love how verse 7 reads in the Amplified Bible. *Let each one [give] as he has made up his own mind and purposed in his heart, not reluctantly or sorrowfully or under compulsion, for God loves (He takes pleasure in, prizes above other things, and is unwilling to abandon or to do without) a cheerful (joyous, "prompt to do it") giver [whose heart is in his giving].*

God loves the joyful and hilarious giver because this kind of giving manifests who He is. God is a giver, and so we should be. God identifies Himself with us through our acts of generosity. I have watched my wife step into the everyday activities of other people. She gives as situations touch her heart, and she is moved by compassion. This compassion has moved her to give money to a lady and her children who were in need in a grocery store. Another time, she offered assistance after overhearing a woman talking to her son in a restaurant about their financial need due to his dental appointment that morning. Many times, after becoming aware of someone's burden in daily life, Shoddy has stepped in to lighten the load. Her constant willingness to be touched by the needs of others has not only brought joy and blessing to others, but it also keeps her life in a constant state of adventure. Shoddy is happiest when she makes others happy. We receive joy when we give, because we allow ourselves to be an extension of Christ to a hurting world. Our joy in giving becomes a reflection of the giving heart of God.

Be His Reflection

The Father's heart is reflected in the ones who allow themselves to become avenues of increased provision for the world. They have proven that they can be trusted with the wealth of this world, and now God can trust them with the spiritual wealth of kingdom authority, supernatural gifts, and divine favor. Since they have proven that they will not waste their earthly wealth on their personal desires, God is now prepared to bestow on them heavenly riches. Our world cries out for this.

I long to see the power and glory of God fill our sanctuaries. It will result in the broken and maimed being healed because He walks in and among us. This is where we see true riches being bestowed—not just in new cars or possessions, but in that which money cannot buy. It is where new hearts and new minds are formed, where shattered souls are restored in a moment of time because of a healing atmosphere created by the generous giving of time, talent, treasure, prayer, and worship. It is in this kind of environment that He pours out His blessings of the true riches from above.

Referring back to the passage in 2 Corinthians 9, I want to emphasize verse 8 here: *And God is able to make all grace abound toward you, that you, always having all sufficiency in all things, may have an abundance for every good work.* I love these words. Read them slowly—*all grace, abound, toward you, always having, all sufficiency, in all things, have an abundance for every good work.* Notice it is not just for *some* good work, but for *every* beneficial work. God wants us full and overflowing. He has things for us to do, and He loves using givers. They are the only people He can really use. Our generosity qualifies us. A compassionate heart maintains that generosity, and according to verse 8, our generosity has an effect on our eternity.

More Proof of God's Will Concerning Generosity

You shall surely give to him, and your heart should not be grieved when you give to him, because for this thing the LORD your God will bless you in all your works and in all to which you put your hand.
—DEUTERONOMY 15:10

And whoever gives one of these little ones only a cup of cold water in the name of a disciple, assuredly, I say to you, he shall by no means lose his reward.
—MATTHEW 10:42

While, through the proof of this ministry, they glorify God for the obedience of your confession to the gospel of Christ, and for your liberal sharing with them and all men.
—2 CORINTHIANS 9:13

Should we not see a full provision and abundant supply of wisdom, peace, joy, health, power, and mercy that flows from us to those in need? Should we not also see the abundance of financial and material things that we have received flow with the same abundance to the world for the purpose of bringing change in the lives of the needy? The answer is yes, we should.

Do Not Just Speak Your Love—Show Your Love!

In Malachi 3:10, God said to bring the tithes into the storehouse, so there would be food in His house. In this verse, He was not talking about spiritual food but something tangible. He was talking about being able to take care of the widows, orphans, and strangers. In this verse, food is referring to something someone can taste, not just something a person can hear. There is a practical, tangible side to our prosperity that people need to see and feel so that they can taste the goodness of God for themselves. Someone in need can "taste" God's love in a blanket, a bowl of rice, a cup of water, or money to rebuild a house destroyed by a natural disaster.

Do not just tell me Jesus loves me; show me something! That is what people are looking for. Do not leave a tract on the table for your waiter at a restaurant telling him or her about Jesus and then not leave a tip. If that is how you act, the only message the waiter will receive from you is that you are cheap. Leave the server a generous tip, and then he or she will read that tract about your Jesus. Nobody is interested in a stingy Jesus or stingy Christians who try to represent Him.

Go beyond the expected! As Jesus said in Matthew 5, if a man asks for your shirt, give him your coat also. If someone asks you to go one mile, go two miles. Always exceed what people ask for! What is it in us that would compel us to give of our time and treasure and exceed people's hopes? It is compassion, a love for people that flows from the love of God. Why else would I deny myself for the benefit of another? In and of myself, I am not that good, but the love of God in me is. Jesus in me is generous and wants that compassion demonstrated as much as He wants to demonstrate His healing power. It is interesting to note that there are more miracles of provision in the Bible than any other type of miracle.

In fact, the first miracle Jesus performed was one of provision when He turned water into wine. His last miracle was also one of provision—filling a net with fish after the disciples had been completely unsuccessful in their attempts. Jesus was always demonstrating the "more than enough" attitude of His Father. Remember the feeding of the five thousand? After that miracle of provision, there was still more left over after all the people had eaten.

A Generous Eye and a Generous Soul

*He who has a **generous eye** will be blessed, for he gives of his bread to the poor* (Prov. 22:9, emphasis added). What is a generous eye? It is the eye of the one who looks for the opportunity to allow what has touched his heart to be released from his hand.

Proverbs 11:24–25 states, *Here is one who scatters, yet increases more; and there is one who withholds more than is right, but it leads to poverty. The generous soul will be made rich, and he who waters will also be watered himself.* I love the way The Message Bible translates verses 24 and 25: *The world of the generous gets larger and larger; the world of the stingy gets smaller and smaller. The one who blesses others is abundantly blessed; those who help others are helped.*

The generous eye and the generous soul are directed by a generous heart, which results in a generous hand. The key to this kind of generosity is compassionate grace that brings change to a situation. The heart of generosity is the heart of the Father. If the great commandment is about loving God and loving people, then it must also be about having a heart for God and a heart for people. Like I have said before, "Love God wholeheartedly, and love people fervently." Only two things are eternal: God and people. If we love God and man, we will also give to both generously. It is my prayer that your prosperous life will be led by a generous heart.

CHAPTER 10

A SENSE OF URGENCY: STANDING BETWEEN THE LIVING AND THE DEAD

Indeed, the "right time" is now.
Today is the day of salvation.

—2 CORINTHIANS 6:2, NLT

Before proceeding with this chapter, I want to take a moment to acknowledge my dear friend Pastor Bill Wilson, founder of Metro World Child Foundation in New York City. The main reason I do this is because much in this chapter comes from his message, and it also has infused within it the heart of everything he preaches. I heard Bill preach this word many years ago in a conference in Hawaii. When I heard it, something changed inside me. I looked at myself in a new way. I was so impacted by his message that I have personally preached it all over the world, not

171

as an echo but as a truth that I continually walk out in my life. I do not know of anyone who lives this in any greater measure than Bill Wilson. My friendship with him has strengthened, challenged, and encouraged me to step into various situations in life and make a difference.

"Making a difference" has become a tag line that we see all over the world, and it is used by corporations, businesses, and ministries. Even our ministry uses it. Yet many of us do not want to risk taking the steps necessary to actually make that difference. Let me ask you a question: Do you think one person can really make a difference? Or is that just something we say to get people to do what we want them to do? Is it just hype, or is it a genuine call?

In Numbers 16, we read a story that will help us answer these questions. It is about a rebellion that took place against the leadership of Moses and Aaron.

> *Now Korah the son of Izhar, the son of Kohath, the son of Levi, with Dathan and Abiram the sons of Eliab, and On the son of Peleth, sons of Reuben, took men; and they rose up before Moses with some of the children of Israel, two hundred and fifty leaders of the congregation, representatives of the congregation, men of renown.*
>
> *They gathered together against Moses and Aaron, and said to them, "You take too much upon yourselves, for all the congregation is holy, every one of them, and the LORD is among them. Why then do you exalt yourselves above the assembly of the LORD?"*
>
> —vv. 1–3

This rebellion, headed by some of the key leaders of the young Jewish nation, was a direct attack on the divinely established leadership of Moses and Aaron. We still see this type of rebellion today where some people are unwilling to recognize or admit that God has chosen others rather than themselves to lead in certain areas. While that can be a tough pill to swallow, we need to get our hearts right and deal with it. Under Moses's leadership, Korah and his crew had it in their heads that they were just as capable as Moses. As we read the historical accounts of Israel's time in the wilderness, we clearly see that no matter what God did, it never seemed to be enough for them. The people were always complaining about something.

Not much has changed since then. Today, people are still frustrated with leaders, and leaders become frustrated with people. Often this frustration is prompted by those who think they know better or feel that they can do a better job than their leaders. On the other hand, leaders become frustrated too, because they may want their people to be more spiritual than the people want to be.

The gang of four, headed up by Korah, confronted Moses and Aaron. They wanted to raise up for themselves new leaders and overthrow the existing leadership. They told Moses that all the people of God could be leaders, not just Moses and Aaron. It appeared as though they were speaking on behalf of all the people, but their words were deceitful. This was a classic power grab on their part. This seditious act had the potential to cause division in the camp of the Israelites. Division takes place when there is more than one vision and results in strife and confusion. And we know that God is not the author of confusion. (See 1 Corinthians 14:33.)

The actions of these rebellious leaders resulted in divine judgment against them. In confirmation of Moses's leadership, the earth split open and swallowed most of the sons of Korah and their households. In addition, a fire destroyed 250 men who had been influenced by Korah. I know we are living in the New Testament age and God's grace is available to us all, but this kind of consequence would surely stop many church splits today.

Now let's continue. You would think that would be enough to convince the remaining people not to mess with God's anointed. Nope! The next day, the children of Israel gathered before Moses and started complaining about the judgment that had taken place the day before. They blamed Moses for the death of Korah and the others. After seeing what had happened to those people, you would think they would have been on their faces praying for forgiveness rather than complaining. What a stubborn lot! Watch what happened next:

> *Now it happened, when the congregation had gathered against Moses and Aaron, that they turned toward the tabernacle of meeting; and suddenly the cloud covered it, and the glory of the LORD appeared.*
>
> *Then Moses and Aaron came before the tabernacle of meeting. And the LORD spoke to Moses, saying, "Get away from among this congregation, that I may consume them in a moment."*
>
> *And they fell on their faces.*
>
> *So Moses said to Aaron, "Take a censer and put fire in it from the altar, put incense on it, and take it quickly to the congregation and make atonement for them; for wrath has gone out from the LORD. The plague has begun."*
>
> *Then Aaron took it as Moses commanded, and ran into the midst of the assembly; and already the plague had begun among the people. So he put in the incense and made atonement for the people. And he stood between the dead and the living; so the plague was stopped.*

Now those who died in the plague were fourteen thousand
seven hundred, besides those who died in the Korah incident.
So Aaron returned to Moses at the door of the tabernacle of
meeting, for the plague had stopped.

—vv. 42–50

Desensitized by the Media

A small group of people with rebellious hearts helped create a tragic situation that led to somewhere between fifteen thousand and sixteen thousand people dying that day. It was brought to a close by the words of one man and the actions of another man. Is it possible to read something like this and not be affected by it? Have we become so desensitized that we can easily read over this narrative without being impacted? It is a story on paper, but the reality of all those dead people might not really sink in.

The media outlets have a great deal to do with the fact that our sensibilities have been deadened by overexposure to negativity and violence on the news and in movies. Nothing seems real anymore! We witness so much death, pain, and poverty that we say, "Oh, well; it is just another story." Things do not really touch us. We read them, see them, and pass right over them. It seems as though we have lost all points of reference. With the increased violence worldwide and all of the natural disasters we view on digital devices, we, as a society, have developed a self-defense mechanism that kicks in to shield and protect us from feeling overwhelmed.

When was the last time you saw or heard of some horrible event that stopped you in your tracks, made you really think, and caused you to take a deep breath or shake your head? Most likely, it was as recently as last night while watching the news. Television programs and even ministries have had to become increasingly graphic in the way they communicate because it has become harder and harder to stir people to feel when they see and hear things. With so much pain in the world, we have built a protective barrier around our hearts.

I have had to learn how to see the pain or tragedy that others are experiencing and humbly balance it with gratefulness to God that my family and I are not suffering at the present time. On the other hand, when I see the pain, hurt, hopelessness, death, bondage, and poverty in which people are drowning, it has genuinely affected the way I look at life and the way I deal with people. This is why I have titled this book, *Thru His Eyes*. My aim is to help you and encourage you to see every situation and person you encounter through the eyes of Jesus. When we look at the world or the people in it, do we see them as Jesus sees them? Do we see what God sees? Are our hearts moved with compassion to bring about change like His is? Are we willing to demonstrate His love to our world?

Years ago, I watched on television as the civil war in Rwanda, as well as the violence that took place in Serbia and Croatia, unfolded. We heard of the murder, rape, and destruction of numerous lives. Pictures of dead and wounded bodies on the ground or floating down a river were displayed over and over again on the television screen. Every atrocity was illustrated in graphic detail. Then there were the horrible images from the tsunami in Japan that were broadcast for all to see. Now with YouTube, we have a dedicated digital video file of every kind of experience one can imagine.

In November of 2013, tragedy hit even closer to home for us as the Philippines experienced the strongest typhoon in their recorded history with winds over two hundred miles per hour. This time I witnessed the devastation firsthand as for months I spent time in the towns and cities that were devastated by the storm. With shattered buildings surrounding us, we walked through the streets and stepped over the body bags of the dead. We even visited mass graves measuring over 110 yards long, 20 feet wide, and 4 layers deep. Somewhere between thirty to forty thousand were lost.

Anderson Cooper of CNN was right there a day or so after the typhoon struck, and the world witnessed the damage and suffering. But after three to four weeks, CNN and Anderson left, and the world was off to view the next tragedy somewhere else in the world. As of this writing, however, we are still here, the dead are still here, the broken are still here, and the shattered cities are still here. Thankfully, the church is also here and is doing all it is called to do. We, the church, are the ones who must step in when others walk away.

Here is a critical question: how many people can we look at, and for how long, before we lose perspective on the tragedies? If we reach a point of emotional overload, we can change the channel so we will not be forced to deal with it. However, as a community of believers in the world today, we cannot remove ourselves from the pain and panic people are suffering. We cannot just "turn the channel" to avoid seeing it. It is still there whether we acknowledge it or not. We are His body. We are to reflect His light and His love as answers to their situations. We are here to step into their world with change.

Urgency Demands a Response

Let's return to the story of Moses and Aaron for a moment. They were watching the people die right before them from this horrific plague. When a person is that close to something, it forces him or her to move, to act. The burden of truth and the reality of life's trag-edies should cause us to respond. When you are surrounded with suffering people, do you experience any sense of urgency? Urgency demands a response!

Moses told Aaron, "Run to the altar." Run. Do not walk—*run!* Why? Because of the urgency of the moment! Lives were in danger, and someone had to act. Aaron was no young guy. By this time in his life, he was one hundred years old. Where did he go? He headed to the altar. What did he do? He took a censer, adding some fire and incense to it as a sacrifice on behalf of the people in order to stop the plague. He then stood between them, putting himself right in the middle of the problem.

Because of the sense of urgency, Aaron ran to the altar. (It is interesting to note that the coals on the altar had actually had the blood of the sacrifice dripped over them.) The altar is to be the beginning place of all action. We must go to there, to Christ, when we want to make a difference. When we make the right decision, it will move us in the right direction. Our standing before people will matter little if we have not stood before Him. Our words will be shallow and our touch will be lacking unless they are infused with the breath and life of the Father. We take Him and all He repre-sents with us to the place we choose to stand.

All of us need to become glorified delivery people, distributing to others what we have received from God. The fire and incense Aaron added to the censer that day represented the presence of God's Spirit and prayers. In Zechariah 4:6, we read, *"Not by might nor by power, but by My Spirit," says the LORD of hosts.* It is His strength showing up in our weakness that makes a difference. Once we know where to go and what to take hold of, we need to go and stand in the middle of the problem at hand. What we carry and where we stand will make a difference and save lives! Moses *saw*. Aaron *ran*. He took action. He stood in the gap, and everything changed.

Do you think one person can make a difference? Aaron proved that the answer is yes. Let me say this clearly: *you* can make a difference! Aaron and the coals from the fire were the only things that stood between the living and the dead. Denominations did not go; congregations did not go; one man went. The same is true to today that was true back then: one person—even you—moved by compassion can save a nation.

One man named Noah heard and obeyed to build the ark. Moses saw, obeyed, and went to Egypt to save God's people. David left tending the flock and ended up saving a nation from the Philistines. Gideon heard the word of the Lord and saved his people. Deborah heard the word of the Lord and brought courage and strength for the saving of a nation. The word of the Lord burned in these people. They were suddenly aware of an urgent situation and took action. Here is an interesting point: God is usually doing so much more than we are aware of, things that are bigger than we could ever imagine.

At the command of his father, David went to see his brothers who were part of Saul's army. His mission was to deliver bread and cheese to them and the commander of their unit. This was a simple act initiated by a father's heart and carried out by his son. However, God had something greater in mind than this modest act. David thought he was delivering bread and cheese, but *God was bringing a giant killer to the scene*. His earthly father had sent David on a mission, but his Heavenly Father had a greater purpose. David heard Goliath's taunting words, just as all the other men who were surrounding King Saul heard, but David's response was different. That day, one man and his God made a difference for a nation.

You and I probably have no idea regarding the thing for which God is positioning us, but our availability opens the door for "the above and beyond all" we could ask or think. If we choose to stand *among* the crowd rather than *apart from* the crowd, we will never make a difference. The majority never did anything. A committee does not make things happen; it is the individual men and women who step forward that make a difference.

Impacting the Philippines

Shoddy and I came to the Philippines to make a difference. It was not all planned out; there was no five-year plan, no job description. Ministry started as we saw needs and began to meet them. I understand the faith it took for the children of Israel to follow the cloud by day and the fire by night. They trusted God each day for direction, not knowing where He was leading them.

In the early years, when we attended Bible school, our hearts—as well the hearts of those around us—just wanted to learn how to minister the Word effectively and follow His Spirit. Have things changed since then? My concern today is that there are some who are focused on building ministries rather than actually ministering. The two are not the same. If individuals will meet the needs of people, they will be shocked at the ministries that will be birthed as a result! These two things must be in proper order. When Shoddy and I arrived in the Philippines, we did not have all the details of what we were to do, but we knew that God had put the Philippines in our hearts. We knew that we were to stand before Him on behalf of this nation. Over the first ten years in the Philippines, we went from knowing only a few people to embarking on a great adventure.

The lack of Bibles and materials for people on certain islands led us to open three Christian bookstores in places where these materials could be made available. We opened two receiving homes for abandoned and malnourished babies and worked on getting over eighty-five of them adopted into homes and families. In addition, we were able to help dozens of babies receive operations for cleft palates. We had a school for street children that began with 5 beggar kids on the streets. It turned into a school for 150 kids in the downtown area where we rented three buildings. It became the best Christian school on the island for grades one through six. This school was later passed on to a dear pastor friend of ours who still runs it today. It has become a school for hundreds of children throughout the city.

The first seminar I held was attended by only 1 pastor, but afterwards, this man began coming to my house every day for four hours. I then held a seminar for 7 pastors, then 13, then 27, then 35, and then 71. Our ability to reach others began to increase each time we stepped out in faith. After a few years, I began traveling around the nation holding a seminar every six weeks. At that time, we were reaching over 5,000 pastors around the nation. We produced a teaching article entitled, *Run with the Vision*, which was printed and mailed every three months to over 7,000 pastors in the Philippines and other Asian countries.

At one time, we had three Bible schools operating in the country that helped to bring forth a new generation of ministers. We worked with all denominations, doing whatever we could to help strengthen the laborers in their churches. We also sponsored five pastors so they could minister on the radio. They reached millions of people with their preaching in various dialects.

Next, we bought our first boat for island evangelism and then another and another. Our last boat was seventy-five feet long, and we used it to reach the islands with the gospel. We traveled by boat to neighboring islands, taking the Bible school students with us while we held evangelistic meetings and miracle services for people out in the middle of nowhere. We also had an evangelistic team that conducted outdoor crusades every month in the cities, towns, and barrios. There we saw thousands and thousands respond to altar calls, as well as hundreds and hundreds of miracles of healing for the blind, deaf, crippled, sick, and possessed.

All of this took place during our first ten years in the Philippines; yet in reality, all we did was show up, see something, and let it touch our hearts. Not knowing what else to do, we ran to the altar and received some fire. Then we ran and stood in the middle of the pain and death surrounding us. Everywhere we stood, we were able to make a difference.

When we moved to Manila, we held a few Bible studies. One of them consisted of three ladies around a dining room table. That Bible study led to the birthing of a wonderful church that now numbers in the thousands. We have a property with a beautiful four-story building on it, as well as forty other New Life churches around the nation reaching thousands of people. We also have one church in Nepal.

In August of 2001, while sitting and talking with Pastor Bill Wilson during the time he was ministering with us in Manila, we talked about all the street children we saw and the areas through which we had walked over the years. This included places like

Smokey Mountain, where people live in and on the dump, North Cemetery, where people live among the tombs with bones scattered all over the ground, the warehouses near the harbor that are filled with thousands of people in one of the most densely populated places on Earth, and, worse yet, the "City of Rats," where children are missing ears or bear scars or craters on their faces from being chewed on by rats while they slept.

It is much easier to talk about these things than to take action, but how long can we talk about them before we make a decision to *do* something? We decided it was time to either step up, speak up, put up, or stop talking about it. We chose to move from intention to action. With that step in January 2002, we, in conjunction with Bill Wilson, gave birth to one of the largest street Sunday school programs in the world, second only to the New York Metro sites that Bill founded. Today we are reaching between twenty thousand and twenty-five thousand children on a weekly basis.

Not only has our church been quick to step in and help after the most recent typhoon, it also has always been there to help when natural disasters have hit the Philippines. In the very first year of our church, we began our outreach by helping people who had been affected by the volcanic eruption of Mount Pinatubo. Years later— in the same year of the big tsunami that killed over two hundred thousand people in Indonesia—the Philippine Islands were struck by a typhoon that killed over seven thousand. Few heard of the disaster because it was overshadowed by the larger numbers in Indonesia, but as soon as we could, we were out feeding, clothing, and providing medical support for those needing assistance.

In 2009, a major typhoon left much of the southern part of Manila under water. There were parts of our area that were in this condition for four to five months. After the tropical storm hit, we passed out over six thousand bags of food to families and over twelve tons of rice. Sometimes our staff walked in water that was waist-to chest-deep. That water was green and black, full of sewage overflow, yet our people took food to those who were stranded. Our most recent outreach took place during the first three months of 2014, where we were working in the area affected by Typhoon Hayaan, the record-breaking typhoon mentioned earlier. We distributed food and building materials, held medical outreaches, rebuilt homes and churches, and fed thousands of elementary school children daily.

Seeing Through His Eyes Is the Key

One of the basic principles that the body of Christ needs to follow is: show up with hands of compassion, and He will guide you. The more you do what you know to do, the more you will know what to do. Too many people want to know how, when, what, and where before they decide to participate. On the other hand, those who see things as Jesus sees show up first. A heart of compassion does that to a person.

Christianity cost Jesus and every disciple He had, yet they gladly paid whatever price was necessary to see His message touch lives. Like His message, ours is not in word only but also in power and demonstration; we must be willing to pay a price to see that take place. It is not a call to convenience, casualness, or comfort, but to commitment, courage, and compassion. Jesus is seen big in lives like that.

I have watched my friend Jeff Perry and Service International from St. Louis Family Church step into disaster after disaster, from the floods of Mississippi twenty years ago to Serbia and Croatia. They were responsible for building homes and repairing the lives of families suffering from murder, abuse, and genocide. They took in hundreds and hundreds of people from New Orleans after Hurricane Katrina who had lost everything, and they showed these people the tangible love of God. I have watched other pastors and churches give sacrificially; through their generosity, they stepped right into the middle of the living and the dead and made a difference.

Stand in the Middle

So many people are disappointed with church and have high expectations of what the church and everybody else should do for them. Have you ever considered that church is much more than what others can do for you? It is a place where you can be trained and prepared to go out and serve others who are in need. As soon as some get a picture of what God expects them to do, they draw back or leave; but let not this be said of you. Are you concerned that you do not fit the part and are not qualified? Well, let me ask you this: who is? There was only one perfect man in the Bible, and they crucified Him. God does not use perfect people; He does not have any. *He uses ordinary folks to do extraordinary things.*

I cannot say that I was really God's first choice for what I am doing. I am sure there are many people more qualified than I am, but what is it that really qualifies any of us? When there is a need, it is His grace, His favor, His leading, His ability, His mercies, and His love that qualify us. We supply the willing heart and obedience, and He takes care of the rest. The most important thing is having God's fire on the altar—not some manmade ambition, soulish desire, or self-serving attitude. What qualifies us to make a difference is simply our willingness to answer the call and go—regardless of our age, economic or social status, race, gender, or level of education.

A Vivid Example

Lois Meyer was a sixty-seven-year-old single grandmother when she came to the Philippines to work with our ministry in February of 1985. She came because she wanted to make a difference. She did not see her age, finances, or family commitments as excuses or limitation. Lois stayed and worked in the Philippines with us for six years. She had no idea when she arrived that she was an answer to our prayers. Several years prior, she graduated from Central Michigan University with a teaching certificate. Shoddy and I had been praying for someone to come who could teach our daughter, who was five years old at the time.

While in the Philippines, Lois also taught in a local area Bible school and started a kindergarten class at a local church. That kindergarten class still continues to this day. During her time with us, there was a middle school next door to the Bible school. The teacher had been praying for someone to come teach the Bible to the students. Again, Lois was an answer to prayer and taught in that school for a season. She also preached at one of the local churches every other week.

Twice a week while she was in the Philippines, Lois would take two girls with her to visit the children's wing of the hospital to pray for the kids who were sick. About those visits, Lois said, "The first time we did this, we just went in and prayed for them all. Then, when we went back the second time a week later, we found that all of the kids we had prayed for had been sent home well and a new batch of children had taken their places."

She came, but she did not stop there. In addition to working in the Philippines for six years, Lois traveled and ministered in Hong Kong for four years and in Mainland China for two years, where she successfully smuggled Bibles on nine separate occasions. Lois also made short-term mission trips to Russia, Dubai, United Arab Emirates, Bolivia, Peru, Canada, Jamaica, Honduras, Israel, Ireland, Scotland, the Netherlands, England, and the Dominican Republic.

Lois did not stop traveling overseas until she was eighty-nine years old. Today she is ninety-six and lives in a retirement home in Oklahoma where she teaches the Bible and ministers to the other residents. Lois just will not stop! I love Lois and how she has lived her life, because it destroys the weak excuses many offer as to why they cannot give, go, or become involved.

Now Is the Time to Act

Many are not able to find the long-range plan of God for their lives because they are not open, willing, and obedient regarding the day-to-day things He speaks to them. They are searching for the big picture when God wants them to start with the little picture, like the people next to them.

Let me exhort you: it is time to show up! Find something to do, and God will honor it. Sometimes I think people want to know what He will honor first. I believe the answer is a heart of compassion. When we get close enough to see the damage and pain people are going through and hear people when they talk about the things that afflict them, it is not hard to do the obvious thing. We are there; we are in it. Aaron was a good example for us; he did what he knew to do, although he had never done anything like it before.

Early in our ministry, Shoddy and I ran to the altar, acquired some fire, went, and found a place to stand. We have never stopped. We have never regretted that decision. I believe the same will be said of you.

Allow yourself to get close enough to people so that their lives can touch you. It is when we force ourselves to get close to the urgency of life—where lives hang in the balance—that we will make decisions from the heart rather than from convenience. The tears, the pain, the need in those crisis moments cause us to realize we are not watching a movie—*this is real life*. People are hurting and dying around us, begging us to intervene. In these moments we have the choice whether to walk steadily in the convenient or less challenging things of life or to choose what I call "long obedience"—those things that take us deeper into the will of God. They connect with us and will not let us go when we choose to see people through His eyes. Through Jesus we have the ability to do something so far beyond ourselves. As the years go by to the place where we have more years behind us than ahead of us, how many lives will we have seen affected by the love of God? As I have said so many times before, you will only bring change to that which touches you. I believe there are places in everyday life where God desires to see your footprints in the middle of someone's hurt and need, as you become an answer to his or her prayers. Oh, how we all need to be an answer to somebody's prayer! I know I want to be; I want to show up just in time when a person needs someone. God wants us to be a light in people's darkness and a joy in their sorrow, to bring them hope when they cannot see a tomorrow. When they cry out for Jesus, how awesome is it when they see our faces because we are willing to respond!

Now is the time for a demonstration of His goodness and His grace. Aaron stood between the living and the dead. He took what he had and stood, resulting in life-saving change. He made a difference, and so can *you!* Come on, everybody! Where are your footprints needed? Look, see, hear, listen, touch, and speak; then watch the miracles that will take place, and see the lives that will be changed through you. All of us together can make a real difference. Everything changes when you see through His eyes.

NOTES

1 Ted Widmer, *American Speeches* (Des Moines, IA: Library of America, 2006), 689.

2 Ben Benjamin, Cherie Sohnen-Moe, *The Ethics of Touch* (Tucson, AZ: Sohnen-Moe Associates, 2003), 108.

3 Phillip Yancey, *The Jesus I Never Knew* (Grand Rapids, MI: Zondervan Publishing House, 1991) 153.

4 Joseph Thayer, *Thayer's Greek-English Lexicon of the New Testament* (Peabody, MA: Hendrickson Publishers, 1996), s.v. "merciful."

5 James Strong, *Strong's Exhaustive Concordance of the Bible* (1890), s.v. "compassion."

ABOUT THE AUTHOR

Paul and his wife, Shoddy, have lived in the Philippines since 1980. Their first ten years were spent in the islands doing many different types of missionary work. These included reaching out through island evangelism, holding seminars for pastors, establishing Bible schools, conducting evangelistic crusades, founding two orphanages, starting a Christian school for street kids, publishing a teaching letter for thousands of pastors nationwide, and opening Bible book stores on two islands.

The Chases have lived in Manila since 1991. A year after arriving there, they started New Life Christian Center; from that one church, they have birthed a network of churches throughout the Philippines. Paul and Shoddy have a passion for the presence of God and possess a heart to touch people with the love and power of God. They have three children: Brittany, Ryan, and Steven.

If this book has impacted your life, or if you would like to contact us regarding our work in the Philippines, please write to us at:

Keys to Freedom Ministries
PO Box 91995
Lakeland, FL 33804-1995

Or email us at: **newlife@newlife.ph**

To purchase Paul's book *The Soldier, the Athlete, the Farmer,* go to Amazon.com. With fresh insight, Paul Chase delivers a timely message for the church. This balanced, scriptural study of 2 Timothy 2:3–6 explains how developing the qualities of a soldier, an athlete, and a farmer—as outlined by the apostle Paul—will cultivate an understanding of the times and seasons, as well as the character, discipline, holiness, and compassion we need to fulfill God's plan and purpose for our lives.